The Garden of G

Born at Narrogin in Western Australia in 1938, Mudrooroo Nyoongah left Perth for Melbourne in the 1950s. He studied at night while working in the Motor Registration Office and the State Library. He wrote *Wild Cat Falling*, and then travelled in Asia and India, particularly in Thailand where he continued to study Buddhism. He later spent seven years in India, three of them as a monk.

Returning to Melbourne in 1976 (via Perth and the US), Mudrooroo worked at the Aboriginal Research Centre at Monash University, studied at Melbourne University and taught at Koorie College. He then moved back to Perth to tutor in Aboriginal Literature at Murdoch University and spent a year writing full time on a Fellowship from the Western Australian Department of Arts Development Fund. In 1988 he lectured in Black Australian Literature at the University of Queensland. He is now working on his seventh novel, the second part of the Wildcat trilogy, and a film script adaption from his novel, *Master of the Ghost Dreaming*.

The Garden of Gethsemane

Poems from the Lost Decade

MUDROOROO

HYLAND HOUSE

First published in 1991 by
Hyland House Publishing Pty Limited
(ACN 005 268 208)
10 Hyland Street
South Yarra
Victoria 3141

Publication assisted by the Australia Council, the
Australian Government's arts funding and advisory body.

National Library of Australia
Cataloguing-in-publication data:

Nyoongah, Mudrooroo, 1939–
   The garden of Gethsemane.

   Includes index.
ISBN 0 947062 66 1.

I. Title.

A821.3

Typeset by Solo Typesetting, South Australia
Printed by Brown, Prior, Anderson, Melbourne

Contents

viii

To
Oodgeroo of the tribe Noonuccal,
Custodian of the land Minjerribah

STRADBROKE ISLAND
DREAMINGS 1989

The Curse

The shouted curse
The wind lifts
Swirls in a twister.
Reaching for the stars,
Uplifting the squall squeals
Rain and sleet and hail
Evading any soft complicities
Of suburban settlements huddled
Hiding from land, dust and muttered
Words of reproach.
Slithering the curse
Agonises on the hot roof
Sheltering the desires
Gone awry
In the shrouded wind missing
My love and I dancing out the storm.

The Beach

Silver clichés the world-beach with moon
Footsteps pacing out the shadows
Smiling upwards at a dead mottled face
Seeking out a discarded rum bottle
Silver-floating, cliché-floating, note-floating
Towards the fish-eaten eyes of that face
Silver-mottled flesh leaching out the moon-sockets
Crated and coated with the aluminium discards
Of another man's leavings on the eternal dry
Beach of the moon never knowing the saltiness of
ocean.

The Bird

In bird-like whistles, I can hear
The slights of you being here, there, or nowhere;
In the discarded revolving door of the sense-filled
Operation needing so faint a push of a whisper
To evade what once I thought we had,
Or lost, or regained – no matter what –
No matter which in that slightness of
Squabbling essaying an inability to please:
A bird leaps off the tree top, hesitates,
Spreads wings and glides away on cliché pinions.

Space

In seeking to essay a line of thought
I probe the space beyond the dreaming
Before the dreaming, in between the dreaming
Words line up to merge into the images
Seeking an answer in areas where questions
Are seldom sought to be evaded:
A vehicle heavily laden with accessories,
Stereo-system, dual thud-breaks, barking
Up the wrong tree, wheels lurching
Along the wreck-scattered sand track of my desires.

Easter Morn

The flatness of my mind
Seeks trees to grow above the red
Pulsing of my blood-vision.
Feeling that the boulders of my mind
Should relieve the barren-ness
Of houses and buildings
I shinny up beyond the pale,
Swing in the sky of crackling boughs
Avoid the slow tumble
For a fast quavering cry.
An eagle stumbles past
As I regain the urge to fly
Beyond the anguish of a sharp roof
Crucifying again Christ on this
Easter morn passing into a Sunday of
Four wheel drives hurtling sand
Beyond the fins of my nostrils.

Walls

Constructing walls
Brick by brick
Layer by layering length
I construct a wall
Higher by highering the flight.
A face peering,
A humpty-dumpty moon-face glowing:
The fall is swift and entire.
The mouth mouths mutterings
About institutions bounded heights
Failing the tunnelling quest
Of desire cementing the bricks
Discovering new impervious materials
Plastering them over and over
Into handsome bulges
Thick and thin and over-indulged:
The collapse is sudden and entire
My body gapes holes
Never to be filled with sighs
Or signs signalling, please trespass.

Constellations

The muddled thoughts of the constellations
Collect the stars into clusters of shopping malls
The trees huddle fearful against the next cataclysm
The clusters break apart into speeding trucks.
I load the trays with star-stuff
Feeling secure that the next passenger liner
Will contain what I do not know
Or seek to know about the labouring engines
Propelling the constellations outwards
To fresh reformations of my desires.

A Mouth

Being formed completely and utterly as a syllogism;
Being hounded and betrayed as a speaking voice;
Being defined and branded by my own words,
My own sex, my own skin, my own tones,
I can only gasp a drying mouth
Uttering silences readily interpreted as an insolence
To be tackled, to be stretched taunt
Into maps and charts of my out-dying breath.
'Hallelujah', there are no more cries for penitence;
But that gasping mouth is disturbing.
It is surrounded by teeth clicking sounds;
It is surrounded by lips dryly rasping:
It may tear, it may suckle;
It may give forth only that ceasing breath,
Smelling of cigarettes and other vices to be pitied
As the good folk busy themselves in forming the headstone
For a grave bereft of body and saving graces.

Minjerribah Morning

Suddenly this morning, this Saturday morning,
This Minjerribah morning, life became young,
Imaged in Bob Dylan singing where else but on the box
As the rain flickered down, as she flexed down
In sadness at just like a woman lying now:
'Everyone will condemn you for your stand,
Of deflecting criticism by becoming great,
A name in faint lights italicised in the pages of history books.'

Today, this morning, I awoke with flying images in my mind,
Seething fancies based on disciples in solitude,
Gloomy feelings whispering of the seeming eternal grey,
A long lightning flash revealed my deserted home,
Then Dylan came singing songs of painful sad glory.
My semen dried on my leg as I rested secure in a knowledge,
That old songs breathe more than nostalgia.

Tracks

Muddy tracks, rain marks end-traces
In runnels, in tunnels, in seethings
Flowing, drifting, edging, turning, oozing
Into the ocean, dark felt-lined by lacy
Identifications in the night of torch-flickering
Faint tracks, lithe tracks, lines of consonants,
Torch-flickering, the pages flickering,
Teething a hard line eliminating.
The meandering track grows trees
And grass and weeds and legs grappling
Burrs and times out of time,
As the track, snaking, twisting,
Moving away into a past of hand writing
Circling about a history of geology
Stratified into emotions paste-like,
Settling down into silt, oozing,
Seething, spreading liquidification;
Settling down, the rain marks end-traces,
As the road cuts straight towards once goals,
Now gone, as that road removes
The runnels, the tunnels in tired dreams
Tarred and cemeted into the solid sediments
Of hard rock dissolving into soft sea.

Style

Moving into the sphere of the personal –
Interpersonal motives of no-fixed intent,
Confusions interplay like old poems to new poems;
Styles intermingle, reflex strategies
Move through words, beyond words, beneath words
In a multiplicity of accenting 'dos' and 'don'ts'
Escalating into a fixed system always being
Dressed up, dressed down, discarded and re-carded
Into decaying systems, evolving systems, never
Revolutionary programs for social increase, decrease
In the moving out-in of the personal
Interrelations, outer relations, fluid imageries
Exceeding or deceeding the matrixes of pain,
The patrixes of suffering evolving, devolving,
Unfixed, always floundering in our 'hellos'
And 'goodbyes' evolving or devolving our relationships.

Movements

In movements gone awry
And lurching to the left
A child dreams dreams
Drifting onto hard rocks
Suddenly melting and clutching
The soft down of your lips
Embracing the thin body
Trapping the bones
And planting the seeds of fear
To enter the pores and itch
And scratch out the tiny shoots
Of fluffy hairs to blanket
A hardness lurching towards a left
At home of nothing doing
But to evade the issues
Renovating the thin surface body.

Voice

In my silent moods running off at the nose
Instead of mouth phantasy thought words
I listen avidly for your voice, to your voice.
It comes in soft underbrush rustlings,
In the guffaw of Kookaburra inaning the sessions
Of my last speech wording heavy straightnesses
Of thoughts which elicit such a response –
A dog barks, gruff and entire sounds,
A finch gives a rapid punctuation
Of terse undercurrents as the sea
Rumbles, rolls, thuds, thunders, rushes,
Incessantly marking out the silence of my days.

Diaspora

The far-flung diaspora of my desires
Finds psychedelic images writhing drug-free
On the slow moving curtain, flesh-coloured.
I calm myself with the crow's craw,
With the steady hum of the refrigerator,
The panting of the dog, the padding of the cat
Driven mad by crazy birds whistling
The hits of the sixties and seventies,
In a passing of the human to the animal
In a thousand glowing eyes essaying to mimic
The neon glow of a city gleaming as a pub
To engorge us, soak up the debris of our sorrows
Then vomit it warm and mellow, fighting mad
About something someone said or didn't say,
Or liked, or didn't like in an angry shout of:
'I'll take on the whole world and fuck it dead!'

Mudrooroo

He came here with a computer
And the broken language of the conqueror;
He says 'No sir', 'Maybe sir'; but never, 'Yes sir'.
His words hit out at the shopping centres and cement.
He desires to turn glass into beach sand.
As a bakhura, he slouches into the suburbs of petty despair.
His words should be treated as the joke of his absence.
Seeking Mudrooroo, they root up his totem,
Bare the ground to dig an Aboriginal cemetery
With headstones scratched by the chains of convicts.
The claws of his toes disappear into kurdaitcha traces.
The tap tap of his keyboard designs
A virus to wipe out programs of destruction.
He raises the flag and watches the grass grow,
And the cell doors open to free all life.
Seeking Mudrooroo in the sap of a tree,
Two hundred years of bloodshed water his culture,
He stands proud, his feet rooted in the earth.

Raining

More seems much less than the grey
Rain drops float, drift, uplift, downfall
With the wind echoing the birds
And the spray-roaring tyres of vehicles
Engineering a fine time elsewhere.
Crow complains, always complains
Though seldom seeking to evade the wet,
The greyness through emigration.
The spirit sits restless tonight
Understanding the fat arses in the pub
Talking clichés of long forgotten mums and dads,
And what a fine, fine time we had
In the sunshine of our dreams
As we sold what selves we had
For the paradise in which we sit
Lightly dismissing what are not our concerns.
We lace our discords with arsenic,
Record them on tape, then play them,
Above the laughing of the kookaburras,
To our children who better their chances
By sniffing glue.

The Mission

The mission shudders under the onslaught
Of Christ gusting, raising a hurricane
Of spread leaves whipped into the backs
Of slaves huddled, quaking in great gulps
Of air rising to merge, racing among the clouds
Of despair shredding the cotton earth
Of desire to spreadeagle the upthrusting pillars
Of the gale erecting yet another tree
For the saviour figure to claim and ascend
In cascades of unknowing the ripped fragments
Of a photograph, destroyed symbol of love destroyed
In a nightmare phantom, symbolising
A destruction equalling the enduring shuddering
Of the Christ descending to rise a pillar of fire
Incandescent with the flames of longing gone astray
In the smiles of slaves rejoicing in the breaking
Of chains breaking the rhythmic structure
Of the mission discordant with pagan chants,
And dismissing it to a heaven within the pale
Of dead leaves whirling, shaking, streaming
In the gusting of creation raising a hurricane
To sweep the steps of our meaning,
Strong, abrupt and entire as a church steeple.

Prisoner

'Prisoner, the cell is secured from
The storms of the forests of the night –
Time madness lurking in a delirium
Of worse than you did to land you here.'

'Screw, secure the house you escaped from,
Secure the windows of your eyes peering,
Locked on the crimes of my passion.
Hold my hand and slip me a caress:
I cruise to flow free from the lurching word.'

'Convict, lock up the anus of your mind,
Stem the diarrhoea flowing from your eyes,
Jangle my keys into the slime of your ears:
Unlocked the door swings free to thud,
Shifting you away from temptation and anguish.'

'Warder, the uniform of your mind shouts commands,
Unlike the wind, it shudders without shrieking
Out the order to let things be:
Lightning flashes between you and me.
We quake at the jumbled signs
Of that great storm gashing blood from stone.'

The Storm

Storm thuds, shakes, rattles, disengages
The ego from fancied studies of antecedents.
Wind pushes, tugs, uncouples the wish
Fulfillment in buffeting waves of rain.
The sand rises sodden to sink back exhausting
The possibilities of relieving distress, as
A sheet of tin glides off to fashion anew
A roof clutched between the branches of a tree,
Sheltering rivulets of water from the devouring
Struggle to eliminate each and everything
In a torrent of thought striving not to be.
Anchored down to race, class and ego
Ridden fancies of a freedom shattered asunder
By phantoms riding high in lusty shrieks of bondage.

Who?

Who knocked at my walls,
Tapped at my door,
Broke my loneliness?

Who came hesitantly,
Conscious of a need to evade
Any hidden intrusions?

Who concealed himself from the opening door,
The spilling of life,
The dappled darkness without
Breathing sighs of a broken love?

Who roamed absurdly around the walls,
Trying the windows, the cracks, the locks
In a sudden confidence of suspicion
At the slight rustling in the undergrowth
Signalling other strangers with other intentions?

Who came and went without entering;
Who came risking all for a single glance,
Then left as the gale dissipated the clouds
And moon light flooded broadly through the senses
To dissipate any issues which might be forced?

House

Those who live in house throw their stones of fright
At naked savages huddled open to the terrors of the night,
Yet never needing all enclosing walls;
Never needing to raise high the roof beam,
Thicken and rethicken the walls,
Bolt, padlock and double-lock doors
Against the fears of the night –
Demoniac phantoms, devils and ghouls.
Never building walls, essaying to created locked doors,
Strange, the savage open to the terrors of the night,
Never needing walls to resist imagined fright.
The night is filled with stars, moon, clouds;
Rain, hail, wind, breezes shifting shadows
Never spirits lurking –
They down in that water hole.

Nicely Done

The waves lash the tired sardines of bodies
Silver upturned, hapless victims
On the sand scarcely twitching
The liveliness of a mind ticking over
With thoughts of trouble heating,
Nicely browned, ready to be eaten.

The sands are littered with bodies,
Unconscious of the boiling sea
Rejecting plastics, glass and steel,
To coach them in with soft murmurs.

Only a few faint shivers betray their nervousness
At being rendered down, made into thick broth
To tempt other tasty denizens like them,
Who wander there canned in 'Have a nice day'
Or, 'Such a beautiful place we'll come here often':
And they lie down to bake nicely done to a crisp brown
For the sea gulls swooping to feast on and enjoy.

The Body

The smell of the sea is a distressed tan body,
Bloated and overcast as the sky at dawn.
Unable to be one with the darkness of the night,
It essays a turning towards, a turning away
Into floodlit gardens of scuttling cockroaches.
Evading any issues of lightened complexion,
Seeking and never finding the dark,
Dispelled by the hot sun streaming brownness
Riddled with cancerous lesions of mind
Existing only as a style, a summer caress
From fingers on the broad expanse of the beach,
It huddles between two extremes spreading blackness.

The Land

The sea splatters me against the land,
Crumbles my body, rips it apart.
I recuperate, push out a pandanus palm.
Roots snake down, touch my skin, penetrate
And hold me entire, piercing through and clasping
Together all my cells as the waves tear,
As the foam dashes against my skin,
Erodes and corrodes, fragments detach,
I fall down, I tumble about –
Still the palm holds me entire
As I flake cells to form new islands.

Unhappiness

The blind hag shudders
The trees twist and fall
Into the rain of unhappiness
Seething at the door in idle fancies
While the wife mimes a lie
Formed for clutching at fathom
After fathom of quivering emotion
Jerking the thought sadness
A small sigh, indeed, into the wishes
Of a happiness attained sometimes
In the faint whisper of 'sun arise'.

Quietness

The felt middle current of quietness;
The constant bass drone of the ocean;
The shrillness of cicadas calling lost lovers
From the harsh croaking of frogs entwining
With the patter of yet more rain,
Suddenly emerging into my whisper
As I sit, a scratch of a pen on a page:
Whispered written words
Not needing the return of answers.
I feel my being entire and complete,
Part of the quietness, the drone,
The shrillness, the croaking and the patter.
Now, not seeking to ask questions,
Just being, here-and-now, while a vehicle
Erupts in anger at skimming over, but never with.

An Old Man

An old man, I fall asleep on trains,
Slobber at banquets, leer after school girls;
An old man, my stomach revolts in spasms,
My feet smell as bad as my breath
Belching fumes of the crematorium of my death
Throes, agony that will eject me out neither man nor sperm.

The Silence

Somehow, the silence seems more intense
Less a missing part of some song called solitude;
Somehow, an absence is felt more as
A presence projecting a past of discord;
Somehow, music seems to mark out pauses
Extending the silence until it becomes a shriek
Of: when I was alone I could order my solitude,
Fill my days and nights with things
Meaningful in their absence of being.
The lacks flow gap by gap into some imagined hole:
A wholeness entire in its emptiness –
Quiet, intense, filled with the catalogue
Of despairs as weighty as air raid sirens;
As felt as that constant sea rumble.
Now, the hole has been filled to overflowing;
I pull the plug and watch the solitude
Tide rise to fill my self with nothingness.

She

When she sails her boat,
When he mutters and hides his pain
Of words slashed across his chest;
As a child is born, grows
And hero-like changes himself,
Or the world he strides,
Along with her breeding in his books:
A dynasty of language beyond converse.

HAPPY BIRTHDAY AUSTRALIA
1988

Presented by the Australian Bicentennial Authority

Authoritative crossbows draw and hiss an English summer sun
Essaying to be Australian, recross-hatching the tropics
Into British shores with reddened skins and arrows stencilled
On the grey cloth of a settlement whipped into streets
Numbered and remembered by scar after scar.
Whitewash flows blood into the darkness, sanctified,
The clasping of two bodies unclasped by undignified
Christianity lightening sad mission faces, the darkness
Foaming, frowning, losing out to the red skin hues
Far from where mummy and daddy were left to die
A bullet riddled death in a suburb called Killer,
Or Murderer, or Rapist, or take your pick
Of national heroes all hallowed by the Bicentennial Committee
Letting bygones be bygones as the shovel descends,
And gold is exported for paper to bribe the wounded earth.
Peace, brother, peace, two hundred years of progress
Is a meandering march of feet treading dust rings over the
Clapped out earth like centipedes reconstituting
A stinging time in the art galleries,
While a child lost and hungry wails
In front of a bark horror-stricken painted;
While a bloke empties his head of all memories of
When we rode, and we done this, that and murdered
The betraying echoes into safe gapped teeth
Of an old codger, an authentic relic of harmless history,
All benign ways and yarns of soft nationalism
Evading any issues of why they rode,
Why they plundered and sent us chastened into
An exhibition where our flag fluttered
Briefly, while we wondered if the next one
Would build such a thick wall
Of thin facts cementing together
Heavy blocks of compressed lies.

(January 1988)

The Ultimate Demonstration

A very important day,
Black and white together:
Beautiful!

Your hands meet in so many faces,
Black and white the ultimate funeral
Waking the injustices of the past
Into a future linking us as one nation.

If all were here, not there,
Together in the survival of 200 years
Messaging the concern for the land.

Hey, Australia, 200 years of birthing a nation
Far older than your wiles.
200 years is less than a piece of shit,
Without curing the ills of division,
Without meeting the outstretching hand
Of those who never landed at the command from a king.

Let us pray: the land is boss;
Let us pray: the land is victorious;
Let us pray: the land needs no birthdays.
Too old to remember the day it was born,
Too old to forget the people it birthed.

Let you understand, our ancientness;
Let you understand, the simple justice of being
Here as the thousands of years move past
In our languages, in our ceremonies, in our celebrations:
Black and white together in a fruitful thankfulness
For our greatness rising and setting forth our unity

(26 January 1988)

Lightning Travels

Dunno who he was, that brother with the hammer,
With the mallet in his fist, just a brother,
One of us mob, who liked travelling on and light
And heavy, smashing his legs, moving his toes, stumping out
A sign for us to follow along behind his ancestral ways.
Always moving, travelling light, pushing out,
Ahead into foreign lands, and hands and arms,
And experiences, lush and barren, flickering with lightning,
Lightning from his hammer, our brother's hammer,
Our father's hammer, our grandfather's hammer,
Our children's children's hammer hammering out.
Namaragan, sweep us together in your lightning flashes,
Namaragan, as my clapsticks mark out the rhythm
Your hammer crashes and in the wind spirit children whisper
Out the consternation of their line, of our line, of your line.

(Stradbroke Island, December 1988)

Talking in Hysterical Voices

1

Inviting a penetration, land seen
as a specific feminine
Patriarchal voices, pricks, horses, pistols
invade, enter, explore
Explode, break, exploit, denude, cover
with the well-taken, well-broken.

2

Old people, fish, water hole, drink,
muttering, broken words –
It seems that they were in some
sort of trance –
It maybe they had nothing to say –
all said, all long time said –
No more, now; no more; long gone, ever gone.

3

Corridor, structural limitation placed
on land,
Unable to relate to naturalness, gaps,
walls, passageways,
Built up, brick by brick, stone by stone,
plank by nailed plank.

4

Language into the naturalness,
language into the all else –
Police stations, high rises, low rises,
mansions, palaces, persons and perhaps –
All words, all languaging
the inability to be natural.

(Canberra, May 1988)

Inside Daydreams and Nightmares

The convict grimaces his aching scars into the smile of beautiful
    Lincoln Town,
His skin eternals the sting of the lash, and yet, and yet a party
On his sadness, on my sadness, on our sadness, on the platform of our
    pain.
Bonza, indeed in juggling old resurrected slang, a convict's creole,
I ache in my blasphemies, a blubbering pain-filled swear-word-filled
Morsel of something unbeguiled by party-time poverty-striken cabaret
Mocking my aching. All I can perform, aches, aches, aches, aches!
I ache, my bones ache, my back aches, my head aches, my eyes ache,
    my feet ache, my hands ache, my elbows ache, my penis aches, my
    arsehole aches, my mind aches, my hatred aches, I ache, ache ache!
So, I have found enough in this historic lurk to demand that the file-iron
    shavings
Of my soul hurt Britain-Australia and those who discovered me,
Though not my ache, though not my pain, though not my hatred.
I have been discovered by this, for this not quite nice stereotypical
Ceremony belittling my failing to call
The kettle black enough to contain the aching of my poor back,
Stretching across Tasmania, Victoria, New South Wales,
Queensland, Western Australia.
Happy birthday, Australia, I ache. Happy birthday,
Australia, read out
My funeral service and smile my aching away
At Britain going, going, gone
In squalor, ugliness and a constant aching from my bones calcified.

(Lincoln, July 1988)

A Righteous Day

A lifetime of inventions sticky-taping a zipper into
A ballpoint pen filled with transistorised tunes
Protecting my wrists from the slashes of insecurities.
Today, I shall hold my head higher than
The kites are flying, swooping down on this
Today, I shall keep my violence passive in anger,
My voice shall be a steel spring coiled.
Today, I shall cut a smile into the provocation of insults.
Today, I shall walk tall with the leaders who walk on
Stilts and stumble as they greet me with cries of goodwill.
Today, I shall stand sober and high under the railway bridge
Echoing and resounding with the slap-slap of straight razors
Stropping on the skin of a year mourning bleeding.
Today, I shall let my fist be clenched in songs;
Today, I shall speech-give the essence of my truth;
Today, I shall be free of harassment and let my steps
Lead me away from the red and black along the golden path
Of the honeyed sunshining of my dreams.
Today, I shall find a will to be responsive to our needs.
For today, this day is our day and don't forget it!
'My bloody oath I won't, mate!'

(Sydney, 26 January 1988)

Too Many Cooks in the Past

New vantage points, new perspectives, the first fleet flying Aboriginal
    flags;
The historians hesitate over the wounded and wrench out nails from
    the deck stairs
Leading to the death of the cook swilling in his bowl,
Digging in someone else's earth, sea-flying-sailing
Into areas where of not the right way shapes
Arguments as to that drowning, as to how best to view
Problems of value devalued, overvalued and submerged
In the seen unseen, lost and sunk in the swill,
Blind to the labouring to bring forth
A bloated carcase,
Structured on human beings unrestrained restraint;
Never striding forth to pepper the police station
With too, far too many skeletons in the cook's
Shall we call it, broth?
Boiling over, unstressed flesh coming from the bone
At uninstructed attempts to escape a boredom of
Points of view, ideologies of undertakers,
And difficult to sort out burial service professors
Falling over them them them them themselves
To prevent fashionable discords
Coming forward to propagate accords
Based on higher salary ranges and prestige.

(Sydney, January 1988)

Outside Conning the Inside Con

No doubt about it, they did lock us up,
Slamming, key-rattling, eye-peering
At our private phantasies passing through their doors,
Their bars, their insanity-inducing practices.
Today, your ghostly arms reach out for a reality-phantasy,
Strive to touch and pass through solid flesh and bone.
Gibber, my hearties, babble, my fine misty friends,
Seek to touch, to lick, to poke, to finger
The saliva dripping over these fine breasts and thighs.
Seek to possess, to gain, to devour our sighs,
To mimic the movements of our bodies inside and outside
This chapel, this house of God solitary flesh-filled
Penis clasped into a climax repeating our coming together
In a blankness of face and emotion so that they will never know
Or feel the present orgasm arching over to unite us
In a communal coming in spite of their beastly practices.

(Lincoln, July 1988)

Sugar in London

We all come here, one time, many times, all times
Staying on in a never ending debate of going home,
Though never going home, dispossessed, brought down,
Left here, abandoned in free will to say on,
Overstay, becalmed, refugeed, overthinking
Our being, creating our stand, denying our ground,
Braiding our hair, matting our inner emptiness,
Filling and overflowing with our imported sorrows,
Or joys, or take your pick, or return for a deposit,
Deposited, once more or never more, over-staying, over-here,
Over-bearing, losing out, emptying out any inclination
To go home, to be the prodigal, the old-new
Returnee with gifts, with knowledge, with terminology,
With harshness, with toughness, with a for rent sign,
Having lost ourselves to the hungry streets,
To the desolation of our private spaces and absent evils,
Vacant of any reason for ever belonging here,
Always of just being here,
A shadowy presence not quite legal,
Though never quite illegal or breaking free of constraint,
Or breaking loose to construct, to build, to centralise,
To remake our being into a fullness of our lives
Forever in this city.

(London, July 1988)

London Reverses the Pyramids

Position the posse,
Grubby hands clutch the empty purse strings untied;
Position the posse,
Clean hands untie the purse strings vibrating with power,
In-and-out pyramid power, no pseudo-cleansing treatments
Meted out to the likes for permanency effacing
The dribble off the cheeks of unpositioned infants.
Unwanted the store closes early on the bleak new morning,
Views and weapons flash representing only a laceration,
Across, in, out, slash me in my falling
At the benefit of warm hands growing coldness,
Dampness of my liberal-sweet, uplifting passion,
Suffering to support,
Supporting in an urge
Not to suffer
The tying of the purse strings,
The knotting of the purse strings,
The vibration of power
Corded beyond the giver
Of laundered money,
Of unspent promises,
Of a wanker eying forlornly
The unravelling threat of images
More real than women's flesh.
In the nightime pubs voices stutter into song,
Feet tramp out a tattered rhythm of patched boots
Whipping the laces,
Whirling the frayed ends of uncaring defeats.
Gone are the passions of the Empire,
Never ever again to be ruled by this dismal climate
Decaying the world into so many sodden lumps of dismay
At the broken promises failing to bridge the fragments of the future.

(London, July 1988)

The Flagpole Flogs the Giant

Motherhood apparently, though denying, the concentric circles concert
Around the propped up virility pole, energised, crackling down loads,
Beneath the blast walls wrathful snarls of proliferating lies,
Shouting, energising, the electric waves shrill out terrified.
Breezes evade the parade ground blurring the concentric circles
    concerting
Beyond the outstretched arms, white, the blast wall deflecting, energising
Lights flickering flags aflutter, weak, limp under the hot air rising,
Ventilation, shafted and filtered the air endures an atomic attack.
Outstretched, the white arms outstretch towards the circles concerting
To a motherhood unattainable, the womb quakes into a safety factor,
And infant-politicians coo and stutter their protests at toilet training,
And their baby wails circle the concentric circles concerting concentration
On the flag pole sagging with the weight of a member too thick
For any aesthetic delights beyond a raucous shout,
    As the concentric circles
Twist and accept a thrust beyond any sky-desiring symbolic
    Capture of the middle earth
And dissolve into atoms designed for total unity.

(Canberra, May 1988)

Killing Sacred Cows

Trying to make a lead, grabbed by the jumper, swinging his arm
The old man's senile dementia lashes the state with a reprieve.
Chaos leaves and yachts attack a child attempting to secure past
    offences
Against the old man for compromising his amicable supporting
    armchair.
Normal prices seek a fall by doubling first a roulette win,
Then tripling it through a great little re-run on old time clothing
Brought on by a drenching in Melbourne's seasonal weather as the
    ships
Batter a vast flood of land prices ever rising after the great debacle
When blacks were done over for a bob or two by ticket-of-leave men
Aching for more than drenching re-runs organised by a syphilitic old
    black fella,
Fighting fella, go-go fella, concrete Neville fella
Haunting the garden to scare the birds with slight silver hair whisps
Famous for a central part, a straddling line
With plenty of room on either side for combing manoeuvres.
Goodbye, old fella. Liberal man got no cause to fight
His woes by travelling suggestions masking a need for
An accountability he never acounted for.

(Melbourne, November 1988)

Failures are Made of This

Phallocratic, never meaning though, managing lies ever necessary,
Moving out, pushing in, withdrawing, comfortably performing.
Phallocratic, but so kind to the living matrix of function.
Phallocratic, measuring success in rising and enduring
The flights of countless times of good intentions always intended,
Sometimes suffered, but always the performance, the satisfaction
In the rising, the lengthening, the hardening – phallocratic
As I've said, built for success when called for in desire,
Always evading, never with a smile, the sudden droop of failure.
Sorry sorry, it never happened before, or did it, maybe, of course.
Phallocratic as I've said. It doesn't matter, though it does MATTER!
Crestfallen, something else fallen too, something limp down there,
Something doesn't get up for the morning shower, something just
Can't be handled anymore, distasteful with insults, known through
IGNORED!
Yes, it does matter; yes, it does, in the limp sour aftertastes,
In the non-performance of certain tricks, in enduring how much
It really does matter to endure. Phallocratic as I've said.
Hell, is an endless slump, though not in the substitute stock exchange;
Hell is an eternity of limpness, of softness, of an inability
To be hard when required, as I've said it's phallocratic.

(Brisbane, July 1988)

Aussie Dreams a Wakey-wake Time

Suburban house wiles the time in fitful dozes of Nyoongah
Dodging how it is as the flowers grow, scatter sleep seeds
Over my faint snores mowing the lawns and stretching out lines
Around the quiet, sunny Aussie dream, fought over
And punched out are the sneerers, king-hit the bastards,
While I hold my dream in my slippery arms, in my limp fists,
In my growing belly spawning the Aussie dream.
A lifetime of nostalgia earthquake lurches into what else
May lurk beyond the insecurity, beyond adventure, beyond the sounds
Of midnight blows sweating out a humid night in sodden wails of
Sound without fury echoing thickly a long lost longing:
I'll sleep under bridges; I'll fuck in store-bought doorways;
My vomit will steam up the gutters; my saliva will fertilise
The parks of this city dancing out flowers from my spit drops,
As I encircle the lowlinesses of old men's rooms and feel
My toothless gums mutter and slime over old adventures
Gone awry in the backstreets of Lima, or even Bloemfontein
As I button my jacket and run to the shadows lurking
With the shifts of yesterday's excuses into tomorrow's penthouse
    posturings.

(Chapel Hill, Brisbane, August 1988)

Aussie Dreams a Wakey-wake Time 2

Suburban house wiles the time in fitful dozes of Nyoongah
Dodging how it is as the flowers grow scattering sleep-seeds
Over my faint snores mowing the lawns and stretching out lines
Jailing the quietness, sunny Aussie dream fought over,
Punching out sneerers, king-hitting the cynical bastards.
Holding on to my dream in my sleek arms, in my limp fists,
In my growing belly spawning the Aussie dream,
Life-time mortgage dream, earthquaking titles to my dream
In which insecurity lurks, in which adventures huddle,
Though the sounds of midnight blows sweeten my desire for
A city street rancid with a beer-smell of wilderness.
I'll seek a bridge to shelter my shivering body,
My vomit will stream away the debris of the gutters,
My saliva will rain down over this city blurring
The dancing lights hazy in my bleary eyes,
Playing over the loneliness of an old man's room
In which my toothless gums mutter dribbling past dentures.
Some folk don't make it to the suburbs,
Some folk one day button their jackets over past sorrows,
Holding out against excessive dreams and penthouse posturings.

(Chapel Hill, Brisbane, August 1988)

The Universe of Facts and Figures

I thought when you said, 'cross', you meant, 'angry',
Said she, said she, staring at the crosses guttered in the stone,
Feeling with one limp figure the crosses etched diabolical in the walls,
The pillars, the archways, the architraves, the plinths.
'I think,' she exclaimed, 'this building is very Hitleresque.'
To be above the human is totalitarian walls extending out beyond
The perspective of two human figures trying for a familiar humanness,
Feeling it extruding, intruding into the hard extensive sandstone walls,
Built up with facts and figures all nice and streaky with disassociations,
With figures clutching scrolls in scowls, clutching bellies
In endless queries directed at the minor's bleak eyes
Surveying Isaac Newton playing with his toys of astrology,
Centring now magnificently the largest of the three lakes
And a parade ground great with the mutters of legions
Of hysterical, thinking thinkers and other grotesque
Stutterers imported from beyond elsewhere where
Progress is defined and escorted here as impressive new styles.
All under the eyes of the bleak watchful minor gilding desires
For mansions and sweet times joyful in the music department,
Playing out symphonies to the funding passions lusting
To serve associated bodies joined together in learned societies.
'I think, that we should leave,' she said, she said;
She said, essaying a slight trembling of the eyes filling the great court.
'I think we should lose ourselves in the desert,' she said, pretending,
That the plentitude around was not desert extending beyond the
    corners of her ears.
'I think I would like to fuck, but not here,' she said moving randomly,
Along the cloistered theories in an effort to avoid an entrapment
In similar circumstances beyond redemption in sand particled stone.

(Brisbane, August 1988)

44

Gapped Sorrow Bridges Yearning

Sorrow, pain, image worshipping withdrawal symptoms until, until –
Wait for it, wait for it, only to plunge again, and again, and again,
The needle icy-touching the skin, pressing in, pressing in, pressing
Through to nick the vein, to nick the vein, to – pain,
Sorrow, aching, withdrawal, seeking an entry, seeking a playful
Time of the needle pressing through, of the tip stinging, ready
To take the plunge, push, push, arrh, uhuh, a shudder, nerve-grating
Sigh hissing the milk through flowing, flowing, disappearing,
    decreasing,
Creeping, inching, pressing painfully through into the pierced vein
Hurting, aching, alive, throbbing, pulsating, a sucking tiny mouth –
All gone, all lost, numbness, unfeeling, blank perceptions blocked
Until the warmth of pain shivers, a maggot of sorrow wriggles
As the vein mouth desires: painful the tiny mouth sucks
Seeking to bridge the gapped sorrow with a tongue murmuring
    yearning
Thoughts towards an empty syringe sorrow-filled and unfulfilled
Without the milky liquid rising finely towards the needle tip
Plunging in, withdrawing, aching, plunging into the tiny mouth
Emptying the syringe as the pain stings, throbs, aches and numbs.

(Brisbane, July 1988)

A Few Eyebrows Raised

Gusted by the wind, dismantled by workers,
Unheralded and unsung the alcoholic upends
A slight breeze to vomit out a castrophe
Of raised eyebrows aping a youthfulness unfelt
Even in the universities of pay-as-you-go education
To be axed in favour of go-as-you-bribe
The undreamt heroes of our cultural misadventures
Socialising in too many junkets to too many cities,
While the boss laughs in his best absolute, golf course
Guffaw: his desires are not our desires!
We sing a swansong in the runes of our discontented
Moaning out some distaff side of our nature turned
Sour with broken promises of marriages denied,
And what we get is what we pay for over and over again,
While those who live and lie weep by on promises.
We lurch and suffer the wrecks of our freebes,
Earth wasn't meant to be nice-and-easy for simpletons.
We suffer the blimp of our minds to descend into their
Economic wiles creating good times another time.
A mother pleads for a missing daughter,
A hotel manager resists the charge,
A policewoman adopts a classic pose on Mother's Day,
In a long trans-sexual howl doomed never to be a mother.
Thank God for small mercies and short sermons,
As we sing and dance amidst our complainer's chaos
Of lies and pride, dignity and understanding edging close
To us and cheering as we fail to supply the solution,
As the romance of Australia drifts past the expo site
Looking for a place to park on a picture postcard.

(Brisbane, November 1988)

Still Bleeding

At precisely one o'clock the copper ball dropped,
Dropped from the top of a mast topping the old windmill;
Precisely on the hour, every hour, the trapdoor drops,
The man, the victim falls through and writhes,
His legs thrash, his penis hardens and spurts
His life away – still bleeding after all this time.
Still bleeding, still ejaculating, still balling,
Still thinking, still writing, still retching
The Indian times, the American times, the Aussie time,
The loony Indian, the drunken Aussie, the melancholy American
Asking what exactly is cooking in the palaces of no-power
To the people? Still bleeding in terror Australis,
Nullness spotted with airfare discounts and what else,
But special limited offers for blood spilt, for sperm
Ejaculated, still bleeding after all these years marked
Out by a now phantom copper ball dropping precisely on
The one o'clock hour in a not-so-hilarious musical romp
Replacing the Aussie burger with the Big Mac easy eating
To appease the worrying emptiness of the hangman's hour,
Vomiting with the soft pap of our history,
Still bleeding in major solo exhibitions of exciting finds
Of when we died and I died and she bled and, wait for it,
Heading towards a future loony, drunken and melancholy,
With creative lifestyles, though poor Fred is dead
To the heatwaves stemming from his lack of structural repairs
To his brain. He never finished his initial inspection,
His additional investigation, his solitary testing of what happens
When your creative lifestyle doesn't match the promise of
The Indian times, the American times, the Aussie times falling
At precisely one o'clock with the copper ball, on the hour,
Every hour with the man spurting his last life away creatively.

(Brisbane, August 1988)

Scraping Brisbane's Etched Sky

Etched against the sky, the python shudders free
To enfold reality in hinged wings flapping aimlessly
At perfection spaced out, at perfection gapped between
Earth and the dark heads of the pigeons encircling
Insistent eyes as the crane flicks out an encoded passage
Messaging relief to the sun-squatters, plastic melting figures
Marking the concrete with an entreaty to flowers to escape
Beyond the cluttered garish positions beneath artificial ribbons,
Streaming out, fluting out those disappearing beneath the rollers
Of yesterday's angels and devil dancers beckoning to ancient fools
To approach this land, to enter this land, to build this city,
Then move on a jig or two to entwine with a toad of misbelief,
Essaying to entrap, or release, or forget, or make believe, or –
Do it, do it, do it, release the crystals darkened with hard crimes.

(Brisbane, October 1988)

Unfaithful Brisbane Night

Unfaithful night, the runes of the city tear at my throat,
Arm in arm, wandering bell-bottoms trace out the petals of deviance
Italian enough to be desired as an antique poniard.
Restless, my eyes query each doorway echoing with my ears,
I seek a sight slightly unfamiliar, but achingly familiar
As the sweat starting on my forehead, wetting my underarms.
My voice mutters at loose passers-by a whimper of negation.
On the lips of their answers, I mumble a hateful tune,
Setting my heart into rhythmically pounding feet,
To where she lies suffering in all the splendour,
Of a door opening and closing on the last flash of her face.

(Brisbane, October 1988)

A Hidden Diary Plague

Diaries, head injurying victims of a blinkered society –
Why, oh why, flowing from my pen, pen, pen to men penned;
Why, oh why, flowing from my pen, pen, pen to men penned.
Judgement diaries moving, moving, convicted by lineal time.
My problems do create a lot of stress in Headquarter's street,
Flowing time filled, inch by creeping inch to when I met the mayor,
Hinting at receiving major head injuries of no, no, no,
The jury shall be hung, drawn and quartered into bank accounts.
Diaries, convicting me by linear time of top people held by diary
Recommending the reforming of the constitution my way, our way,
Believing always the glamour boys get better with every entry.
A slight mishap as locals conduct a street pray-in for the lady
To beat the regal plot to break the black day isolation blues,
Uniformed by me seeking a chance to score a holiday for services
Smiling at the villain demanding superior salary beyond my means,
As he exposes my family history creating a new blotting on the diary.
At my place, the time, the flow, the ink, the pen, the pencilled
In squares of my doing the undoing of my phone-in lunch reaction
Denied, contrived, and given mixed blessings at the prayer meet.
Why, oh why, cashback offers are denied with my convicting pen:
You simply can't get the dirt, grit and stains out of the force,
Classical wooden heads though a lot are old blokes there aging,
With a yen for easy money on a plate: It's painful, you know,
But feel the fear and do it, do it, do it, anyways until tomorrow
When the diaries stop at how many positions I could think of,
Think of, do it, do it, without a diary, diary entry,
Tearing me apart, writing me apart, putting me together into the top
Bracket, racket, pack it and enter it in the diary, diary
Diaries, smarming the underpinnings of structural disrepute;
Diaries, warning light fittings revealing serious innuendoes;
Diaries, you know, I value money more than, more than, more than,
A diary entry positing how much I won at the race course,
Winning country-style with dynamic techniques crammed with
    briberies.

Crammed with knights and dames and entrepreneurs and books made
   over
Not forgetting, though maybe too old, hey, excuse me,
Final diary entry if you please –
Please me and read this last heritage message:
It's formally fantastic,
Diary stopping with these lines:
He said that the police force needed me as a strong honest
Commissioner
To rebutt
The nationwide attacks on the integrity of unbalanced reporting
In the diary, poor poor me in the diary.

Brisbane, September 1988)

Getting Off My Knees

Transports help me, bring me home as a priority
Replacement worthwhile to find the guide line,
Double or single wheeling.
I was hurt as I went through the secret pathway while
Languaging a mouthful of promises, ready –
Set and gone to the knackers.
'What do you mean,
What do you mean paying the wrong wrong 'un?'
'Arrh, just a complete fast delivery,
A precision surface centring
And shaping while fearing –
I was being setup for money backed promises!'
So much for conversations,
Threatening action on power structures,
While feeling that it means more than a dog-smiling device
Embedded in the crevasse of a hairline fracture.
Baldness, freeing the scalp of such hairy adventures
Shocking and smashing while taking a back seat
Though I do mind the taking of any seat anytime.
I resent the loss of the speaker,
Support veteran primary protection
Falling short of the listener listening to one side.
'Hah, hah, hah,' his voice stutters out short bellows,
An old yarn spinning out a tangled web of deceit.
A petrol drum flashes under the stars,
The head behind the face wrinkles, strives,
Questions mysteries of ambushed conditionings
Achieving something,
Guarding something,
Talking over something,
Remembering a time of understanding without a promissory note.
I had the gold, the diamond in the mine.
It was all right, right!
Now uncaring, now contracted to success and the death penalty,
That's all right, I had it.

Familiar hands miss my shoulders,
A familiar mouth splutters T.V. words radiating colours,
Self changes his clothes for my respectability,
Goes out and does a bust,
Hoping to be treated as a dog,
A leper,
A face of torture sobbing;
But no, on my knees I huddle and try to hide neglect
In jazz and blues and rock the emptiness between the players.

(Brisbane, September 1988)

Stressful Signs for Sale

An urban drill, the face distrusts the song the ear mushes,
Horns blend voices shrill the discord of urban drilled
In colour combinations combined for elegaic events
Of stiletto heels grinding down on glamour screaming:
'Hello,' into a drum solo hiding any pity for the crippled dwarf
Mocking a face at the stressful comeons signs
Fabricating hardons over a shopping village
So organ blowing, a bazaar of health and with fire exits.
Even a car intrudes to extrude the fumes of a perfumed prize
Under the steady lights flashing out chicken-winged fancies
Of absolute pure delight, shards of the ultimate taste experience
Shattering and glittering, reflecting and emitting voices deceased,
Now distant, now near, near, near, near, right next to the dwarf,
Me in jumbled, distressful, disjointed, Chicken Little here ate this
    mourning
In midget gulps of exciting lighting dazzling streams in the female
    toilets
Aglow with the stainless steel urinals glimpsed through the men's
    rainbow doorways
Of broken pints last night as the stream hesitates over a few weak
    reddish drops.
Stressful signs of the dwarf gone ape over fire proofed candles
    remaindered quality
On which I blow and blow a flare into my reflected image,
Glinting off the tiled roof, off the glittering glass, off the 'Buy Me
    Pleases';
And I, myself, mark me with a price tag in a half price sale of midget
    merchandise,
Somewhat out of date, somewhat shop-soiled, somewhat out
Of true in this giant-sized shopping village.

(Brisbane, November 1988)

Arrested Development

Arrested for being public in a public place;
Arrested for saying freedom is not mine;
Arrested for sniffing out the pigsty.

Arrested development burns into the hotel,
Renovated shoddiness falls on the publican's head,
Felt fingers glide past his throat,
The gap-toothed mouth smiles at the tourist's pissing
Past a little fear of not coming here for this
Incarceration of lost hopes in the French pavilion of New Caledonia.
Don'cha know they lie in their bootstraps torturing to death
Liberty, equality and fraternity under the same old horrors
Of the red, white and blue-veined frog feast.

Arrested for marching to a different tune;
Arrested for marking out a place too soon;
Arrested for daring to reveal my face.

Scuttled Labor enacts no revolutions today,
Or ever, jobs on the line and over the line,
Done away with, redundantly certified as bossman's wiles.

Marx the time with unAustralian ideologies define
The next stages of Capital exploitation exploiting
Everything, but Labor not required or worth denying:
Cut, blame, count, remand, instant writs revival
Somethings which happened almost a century ago,
Not yesterday and the bossman still over we,
And all our tomorrow's sold, sealed and delivered,
Inspite of Labor and their party politics galore,
All establishment-suited and fuck-over us.

Arrested for not keeping the red flag flying;
Arrested for unsmiling face their lying;
Arrested for not walking at their pace;
Arrested for stepping into our place.

(Brisbane, September 1988)

The Bagman 1

Hey, hey, the bagman, bagman, slagman, know him, can him,
Barrister charges pistol replication,
Judge's son jails boy, lost in the channel
Of the bagman, bagman, no violent action
Reaction to mother blasting leniency of the fraud doctor –
Bagman, no police threats to the killer bagman
Taking to the air, escaping the probing
Of the royal chambermaid's dirty linen – excuse me,
Excuse me, hey, hey the bagman.
The Aussie style for the next new year,
The knocking knocker knocks the church –
Cost scandal of non-users paying
For the gender relevant to city hall bagman
Entering the workforce of the hangman, hangman bagman.
No other choice but the bagman, hey, hey the bagman.
Promises upkept for property invested with the bagman;
Other choices up for the bagman, extra features,
Extra costing, extra cheap, renovated and stylish
Is the bagman burning cannabis to fill his bag-filled
Heroin addiction, nodding out and over the whole world
Of the bagman, hey, hey slag the bagman.
Our service is expert and Australia-wide,
Lease, rent, or buy your own backside,
Take home your own sunshine.
Nation set up to crash with the bagman,
Bagman set up to cash on the nation,
Reaching out and tendering a surplus taxation.
You and I, and cops and robbers,
Church and steeple, and sexy dollars,
Whisps of chicks and elegant fairies,
All for the bagman, bagful for the bagman,
Bagman, hey, hey the slagman.

(Brisbane, October 1988)

The Bagman 2

Hey, hey, the bagman, bagman, slagman, know him, can him,
Barrister charges pistol replication,
Judge's son jails boy, lost in the channel
Of the bagman, bagman, no violent action
Reaction to mother blasting leniency of the fraud doctor –
Bagman, no police threats on proposed charge probe
Of killer taking to the air in an escape bid
For the royal bagman stirring dirty linen – excuse me,
Excuse me, hey, hey the bagman:
The Aussie style for the whole new year,
The knocking knocker knocks the church –
Cost scandal, non-user's shouldn't pay
For gender not relevant to city hall bagman
Entering the workforce of the hangman, bagman.
Death penalities aid the bagman, hey, hey the bagman.
Keeping no promises for property invested in the bagman,
No other choice but the bagman,
Extra features of the bagman,
Extra costing, mighty, cheap, stylish, renovate
The bagman growing cannabis to fill his bag trickling
Our heroin addiction paying who else, but the bagman.
Take the whole picture of our advice,
Our service is expert and Australia-wide,
Lease, rent, or buy,
Take home your own sunshine.
Nation set to cash in on the bagman,
Bagman set to cash in on the nation,
Reaching out and tendering for surplus commonwealth property.
You and I, and cops and robbers,
Church and state, and air and water,
Whisps of chicks and elegant fever,
All for the bagman, bagful for the bagman,
Slagman, hey, hey the bagman!

(Brisbane, October 1988)

A Flower, A Weed, A Tree

A flower discards the blooms of a weed beside a dying tree,
Survivors of the holocaust come to see all there is to see,
Tropic forests clinging moonshine lit as lights flicker
Out neon blossoms edged along a sculptured tree. 'So lifelike,'
The tourists cry in their beers dribbling along to marvel
Over a flower discarding weeds as it blooms on Expo's shoreline.

A suited person ties one on in the half tones of a reddened lily,
Emasculated beside the topical sight, he poisons it with laughter,
As the flower dissolves into a blonde having to endure the slaughter
Of a profitable time for all the discarded weeds to die
Beside the dying tree-line of the building slime-line sawed
With spikes of flags flying dripping from on high the rotting seed.

Above the swatted fly struggles to rise on the hot air of voices,
Aiding a bus to pitchfork its nose as royality ambles
Up to surround a pole, a moving glimmer of switched on smiles,
Holding steadily to no man's hand, the helicopter splutters
Out release to veterans safe asleep in god's willing paw,
As an old lady goes 'whee' wheel-chair gliding to the dying tree,
Plastered with get well messages, and welcome to the world, good
    buddies.

And in the circles of an 88, appearing and re-appearing in what we like,
The heavy engine groans into the fluttering weed heedless of the night
    asparkle
As the gleam, fond-farewelling of my true love's loveless eye-ball
    bright
As she stutters, 'crass', thus evoking plastic and dazzle to engage in a
    fire fight,
Of 'What else can we show the world, but the imports of ourselves!'
And beckoning to the plane, you escape to the right of heaven's gloom.

And I do not greet you, yet I do not not greet you,
The bondage of my sighs mops the morning too hot
For trivialities, energy expended in cheery smiles,
Yet I fulfil the need for an advertising company
To scatter the torn petals of caring to dismantle
All ill-feeling, I might have towards that dying tree-
Lined alleyway down which you take me smiling lies
Aimed at goodwilling me into lapsing down my guard.
I never cared for the weed of your love, my dear,
Though I shorten and expand these lines recklessly
Into a need for your lips and hands yet again,
And again, for every morning is a good morning
Yet again played out on the tune of 'Who's Sorry Now.'

And in my scowls, my bloated belly, a psychedelic sail fills
Stars into a sack loaded with my incredulities: I never saw
The likes of you and you in the snarls of my downtown parking,
Asking for more and more than I could give in firework displays,
And lifeless dummies planted to deceive that I am wrapping
Up my sails, dissolving into my rainbow hues while attempting
To believe that the here-and-now is an echo of my dreams heralding
A dawning of a day of many colours, a perfect television screen
Framing the flower, the petalled weed pressed against the scarred tree.

I have attempted to be with you in a post-nuclear wonderland;
I have become part of your voices exclaiming 'sorry' and 'pardon';
I have missed you in your suicides and early departures;
I have counted my money and scowled into your good graces;
I have planted and built all that I could dream in my dreams;
I have let the side down by the vastness of my fragility;
I planted the flower to watch the petals deform into weeds;
I erected the tents of my hopes to flood out the cries of the dying tree.
I am not what you call 'good' or 'bad', only ugly and indifferent,
Never mind my numbness or attempts to shift evasions of the spirit
As my sails fold free to protect the earth from any exorbitant fees,
Just as the blaring of my bands tempt you to sing along in semi-tones.
My 'all the world's a stage' is filled with humanity,
All whom we asked came, performed and left leaving me entire.
What more could I ask for, or endure, or live up to
And see it flowing once again in a future birthday of my race.

(Expo Site, South Brisbane, December 1988)

In the Garden of Gethsemane

Staggering across the stars, the parking lights,
The rushing, gaoled head lamps,
My mind is drunk with my blazing past
Searing my body towards an awesome destiny.
Alone and distraught, I erupt into the sky
Twinkling a soft nursery rhyme into my agony.

In the shadows, I hide fretful with indecision;
In the shadows: 'Father, take this chalice . . .'
Darkness weaves gleams into a crown of thorns;
Disrupting voices mock at my drunken steps,
Sinking down, I tingle: it is to be, to be,
And yet, and yet, the beam of light outlines:
It soon will be: the body hanging from that tree.

The spotlight flashes the police car siren
Marking out the diamond blackness of my road.
Laden down, I stagger a drunkard to his sordid doom,
Where four X's spell out my words of love,
Echoing sadly in their fists and thudding boots,
Then someone comes with a crown and robe,
They laugh, anoint me 'King', then murder me.

(Toowong, November 1988)

Enplaning With a Smile

Extending out her smile beckons beyond the city roadside shopping
    arcades;
Beckoning, her uniformed wrist swirls a circle of thin gold around
    thin bone;
Lost, the exit seems to appear marked out by a blue line ensconced on
    teeth marks;
Seeking an entrance, a baby cries out some sort of solution to the
    thunder
Punctuated by a gong-beam signalling out a time to be aware,
As the wheels infold into faint music disappearing into a maelstrom
    wheezing out
A gleeful beeping 'Beware, beware' – strap down your phobias
    and undo
Your mind fright-flight afraid to be unafraid as her smirk wills you
To ignore any felt vibrations of sudden catastrophes.
Falling down, falling down, falling down,
You rise to pulsate, free again, yet alone
Again in the hands of those who palmed your mercy,
As they begged for something with wings and a tail.

(July 1988)

Again in Melbourne Fair City

When I was here last time, a soldier held back the wall,
Doing my undoing, his back a deluge of icy flowers,
Cold and white, dissolving in a slick rain stream.
That last time, the soldier hard and abrupt with me,
Obeying his fanciful orders, the world collapsing around him.
Now in the debris, my broad back lies flat to the sky,
My tongue laps, a tiny pool of muddy water eases my thirst.
What do I miss, my scars mark my inexperience,
My body shudders, ever to be in doubt,
'Doubting Thomas', a black-robed figure flings at me
The taunts of my childhood, parasitical I seek a love,
Pressing the dark girl beside me, pressing the inadequate me
Agonising over past mistakes, the last vestiges of hope murmurs,
My mouth smiles, distressful events strengthen the soldier,
Never relieved, obeying always the callousness of those last orders,
Refeeling that last cold handshake, his duty reels in his mind.

(Melbourne, November 1988)

Church and Steeple

In a Hitchcock film, a man falls from a steeple in dream,
A woman falls from a steeple in dream, a man falls from
A steeple in reality, falling as the woman does from reality:
Vertigo of stone walls, marble halls, slabs of concrete
National thrusting into monuments for a new year cracked like
An old pillar cemented into a young-old fellow as race memory
Turns into a confencing hall stockyarding a missing deity
Receding, receding, seceding, winking out in a spotted floor flag,
Winking out as an eye clang, a system dismantling, collapsing,
Nature re-addressed in preservative, fenced and framed
While the eye whispers shut, the lash hairs spraddle the crenulated
   ceiling,
As a voice hums through the eye, now beyond the whisper enduring
Quietly, softer and softly, a straining of the ears to recollect
The last memory drops dripping sound into the last fluttering eye lash,
As what once was vanishes beneath plastic sprayed over the skeleton.
In a Hitchcock film, man-woman falls from a dream;
In a Hitchcock film, man-woman falls from a reality,
A steeple, a church, a spire, an eye, an ear, a voice –
Vertigo – a dream falls from reality, a reality falls from a dream.

(Aachen, June 1988)

Talking Author

Sounds, rough gruffnesses where women enter slightly tittery,
Slightly kowtowing to engineering the hidden preserve of masculin
Deep within the machismo of switch blade buttons modelling
Shorts and tee-shirts gleaning a now freedom from the job
Futuring things, the program slips into place quietly.

A novel is a middle-class European constructed as a dry dream
Hiding the bleariness of earth-seeking cultures never writing
The spiritual yearning styles evading the alienity of this my form
Unchosen, yet seeking to express seasonal changes moving past
The stranded individual feeling flooded and tree-felled.
Lost the ancestral hero hesitates to mark out a standard,
Forsaking the moment to let through the present futurity
Fortresses of where we are, the dreamtime flickers fine fire.

At the place of the Two Men;
At the place of the Iguana;
At the place of the limbs rubbing together,
The honey grows, flows thin.
At the place of the Two Iguanas,
The snake crawls free and drowns in honey.

Clear evocative prose squirming it crawls like smoke
Marking position with rising influences blunting the fangs,
Broken, rejuvenating, the placement of religion
Illusions, a return solidified into mad houses.
The rifle is lifted, emptied, dropped from
The passive hand, fingers unclutching, clutching nothing
Spasmodically, the volition endures and suffers defeat.

I have seen, I have seen the expanding of topics lost
In the grunting of a pig – real, the blunt-nosed fellow
Snouting out the goodies in sub-atomic particles;
Puzzling over questions repeated only by tramps
Absurdly browsing in the University, tea-shopping
In the bookroom for random static moments

Between the shelves, between the shelves hiding dusty
Unimportances in the central western defeats encountering
The absurdity, the universe, a hedonistic whine.

Soul-feeling that in my orgasmic moods raped by feeling,
It's there, there find it in hindsight in an early review
Lounging with the characters lounging within the author.
Painless and circular, the pattern patterns the organism
Numbering the end, the outside leading from and into the inside
Running through the gaps to belong in an elsewhere
A gunyah which is never folded, but left to fall back
Into the earth, through the earth, under the earth,
The stone gunyah waiting for the growing within.

ngaija been yaan,	*(I come,*
naara been yaan,	*Dance comes,*
woordoomanoo yaan,	*Brothers come,*
naara been yaan,	*Dance comes*
Mudrooroo been yaan,	*Paperbark comes,*
naara been yaan.	*Dance comes.*
yandaara gwabeen,	*We give the food,*
marra yanga gooling,	*You give ornamentation,*
beerart gwabeen.	*Soft fur whitening.)*

The growing in, the piercing through prickling skin,
The dance holds old memories stone-free from stone-cold
Fur strengthening thoughts with pipeclay designs.
And my ceremonies are my words dancing lines,
Fleshing out the boro grounds with the dream image of the
    Stone gunyah.

(Brisbane, October 1988)

Oldering

The not quite right suit, the not quite right trousers,
The not quite right times of oldering out the seasons.
Now clinging desperately, now greedy, now a psychic drooling
At what has been missed. Private eyes drop away from the video
Images forming a hooded cliché figure with a sickle.
Essaying to believe that death comes like the man in the mask,
Like Yama riding on his black buffalo plodding towards –
You won't believe it even when you're there in the ruins;
You won't believe it when the old man beckons to you from
The dark tunnel of his wurley. You won't believe and doubt
That this is your last home. You defy the death brutal attack.
Killed by train, killed by plane, killed by car, killed by home
Tragedies, done in, fallen in towards the water hole bracken
Surrounded by the pitiful aching years of rubbish self
You clean and clear these rancid waters for the death jump.
Oldering, clinging, greedy, a thousand thousand year lotus
Closes over the grey head in sleep expelling times of later on.
Oldering, the light flickers, grows stronger, blazes in mists.
Oldering, Jack Davis's dancer dances towards you his face,
Old Worru mutters in his fitful sleep, then quietens down.
Oldering, fervid fancies turn tolerance-laden towards earth things,
Love tears relieve as you fall beneath the surface of the water,
As you mount the buffalo, as you evade the sickle for the lotus
Covering you for an eternity of sleep, or nothingness,
Or what might have been as a vacancy not even signed with your name.

(Brisbane, August 1989)

Lost Love Hovers Near

Never seeking, yet finding, never yielding, yet soft
In the permutations of your frown, I seek your smiling
Face beside the waterfall, that day when we exchanged
A brief greeting before a simple parting at the station.
Yet the train never came and never came for us that day,
That night, that morning lost in the hissing flight of
Rainbows rising only to fall into your sigh at the sound of
That hissing, of that serpent, airliner engines all astruggle
To separate us into distances and far aparts and see-you-soons
In the battleship scars of a new tomorrow bereft of that
Rainbow sign, the never arriving train, and our few thoughts of
The morning failing to bridge this our future separation,
Now present and pregnant with a future pregnant with you.

(Brisbane, August 1988)

Time, Lady Time

Fractured relationships slither past ruins,
'This is my life' flashes up a grin of farewell.
Institutions raise walls, placards spell out,
Arrivederci to timeless dreams of intimacy living
In ancient myths of being born for each other
Between the beckoning walls of an old man's flat,
Where he routines triumphant Boy's Town discipline.
Massive with candle lights he celebrates a dinner
For his release from the tolling of the Angelus bell.
Now his life is old men playing chess in a warm park,
Then exchanging a farewell, they retreat to burrows
Smelling of the flatulence of their old rituals,
Learnt in that Boy's Town, self-dependence no need
To please any groping hands, or love demanding minds,
Trapped in unpleasant scenes of a tedious relationship.

Time, lady time, I am capable of managing
My own plantations of the forms they seeded,
When they thought that they owned our kind,
And grew us up to make believe practices
Latent with the possibility of never harvesting
A crop of our own seeding and painful growing.

(Brisbane, September 1988)

Waiting Time Out

Once I wrote a poem bout a waitin time,
Wrote a song bout it too:
Waitin for you, waitin for you,
In old Country an Western corn:
Was I waitin for you then too?
Eyes brighten at the fickleness of my spirit,
Now mournin in that blank time, in that void time,
That achin time laden with gleamin figures sadly
Playin out a solitude in a mind twistin with
False images drained of a time even before the waitin,
Before the you were here, and now you are not –
Feelins that form, that elevates these images,
These phantasies pressed not from life,
For without you,
The stream of images flicker by unowned and unattached;
For without you, a sunrise reaches up and descends without a qualm;
For without you, a hurt mind hesitates over the pinpricks of hope;
For without you, time bends round and nips my nipple to the blood –
And you aint even here to taste its saltiness.

(Brisbane, August 1988)

Poetry Giving a Recital

For Cilla McQueen

He stretches feet at the audience, leaning back an elevated face
    attentive,
Listening to the strands of red-hair bridging the mouth towards dark
    legs,
From somewhere, in between, a voice begins, calm, clear, uncaressing
Images misting the occasion as seen through that red-hair
By a half-dozing pussy cat awakened by saddened city cries.
Stone womb swords stir free as a heel shatters what remains of the
    block,
Then silence, then words begin to read from the crevasses of history
The reasons behind the sword of that shattered stone womb.
Pebbles raised high into castles in New Zealand, in Perth,
Sydney, Melbourne, each possessed with a simulcrum of the sword,
Of time dialling out a different time as my eyes watch
The hands creep through the lyric sounds – voice murmuring
For and against the sword, the stone, the block, the pebbles,
The simulcrums disenchanting, declaring, unbinding the spell
Casting forth the reasons of why I have not succeeded in meeting
You face to face in the full gaze of the sculptor and his blocks
Of tassels swaying towards a voice now ceasing in applause
At
The ending
Of a poetry
Reciting
The triumph of the sword,
The stone womb
Blocked out into words
Falls sweet
Into an enchanted
European hall
Rich with clichés
Of old ghosty monks.

(Aachen, June 1988)

Relating to a Bourgeois Painting

Shall I, identify painting, done by, framed by
Someone who watched Mr Man on the prowl:
A figure skater, well kept-up, propped up by dignity.
Hands in pockets, shirt-front neatly arrayed,
Eyeglasses winking, crafty eyes gleaming coldly at the prey.
Pray the prey, coins rattling ribcage skeleton,
An endless pinning of the tail, tailess wonders
Beside him reduced to turnips, green-tipped,
Sketched in hurriedly, dismissed by painter and hunter.
Cold eyes gleam, grey hairs flutter in his nostrils,
Stained tobacco fingers fly at the figure skater,
Reducing him down, machismo's doll, rough-sketched strokes.
Hurriedly the crayon derides reality in straight lines,
Deciphered, delineated, the stalker stalks his prey.
Pray who is the prey? The painter daubs in the quarry
Gossiping together, the grey moustache quivers,
The hands deep-pocket-thrust down
Into the lines of the sketching crayon,
Into the lines of the sketching crayon.

(Amsterdam, June 1988)

Faces Stare Into the Gaze

My gaze slides smoothly without a simile for feelings,
Laughter erupts, the floor shakes, faces avoid my gaze
Moving up the stairs clinging to plastic shoes ascending,
Clinging to leather shoes tripping over the back stairs.
My gaze glances, recoils from faces pushing eyes towards me,
To catch a glimpse of my gaze avoiding their gazing,
Harshly seeking out a sign of acceptance,
Responding to in a clapping, applauding a release of tension.
If looks could kill, I could launch a thousand poisons,
Swiftly, deadly, silently, if looks could kill, kill, kill,
I'd bottle mine and let them drip forth as spiders
To dart about, pose as poisonous glances,
Then spin a web sticky with venom.

(Brisbane, December 1988)

Movement Pushes Out a Little Thought

Movement pushes out a little thought
Fretful and unused to the wiles of caresses,
Meanwhile in the bars the men line up for whisky,
And lift their glasses above all feminine care,
Celebrating in the rowdiness of an obscene singalong –
In my home, my house, my garden of careful scrutiny,
I moan along with the carelessness of your smiles.
Teeth bared, shovel erupting the earth,
Weeding in spasms the retching jerkings
From my body, as the stations of the night descend,
And I miss the hum of the lawnmower,
The fart of a vacuum cleaner cleaning cleaning
Out and out and out any hopes of living
In the morrow far beyond this dream of flesh and ooze.

(Highgate Hill, October 1988)

Mutters the Stuttering Movement

Static enough to appear to be an unmoving essence,
I let thoughts flicker, flicker past eyes unseeing
Beyond last night's unforeseen non-invitation
Echoing a tunnel closing in on all the unthought feet,
Never appearing, or receding, or sounding out a 'yes',
Or 'No' as I turn away from any abject movement.
Muttering just enough to enter the peering of my senses,
I excavate a sacred site, enter through and extend
Far from here to erupt as desert snow, senseful,
Senseless of the ocean spiteful enough to drown me
In a rising snigger at being unable to understand,
Or listen to non-moving feet in an enclosed tunnel
Large enough to watch the snaking serpent turn back
Bite and bite and fang my movement stuttering static
Thoughts into an unmoving essence coil upon coil.

(Stradbroke Island, December 1988)

Everytime Flickers the Archetype

It flickers, flickers, flickering, a spiteful flicker,
A constant flicker, a corruption of the eye business,
In front of my eye, behind my eye, side on to my eye.
Flickering, flickering, child's flesh burning,
The stone knife, the slither of glass, the slash of –
Flickering, the hateful teacher's hateful strap flickering
An adult hand to pump pain into the shivering me of my flesh,
All quivering, all shivering, all flickering, flickering,
Collapsing, enfolding back into an archetypal flickering.

At rest in the archetype, flickering,
My shivering flesh,
My burning skin,
My fretful mind,
My lacerated soul,
Flickering, flickering, flickering
In tune with the archetype flickering.

(St Lucia, November 1988)

Moongalba

Is it named after the moon, suffering lover's cross to bear
Amongst the betrothed pines, palms, eucalypts, people walking,
Muttering low incantations aimed at desertion.
Sweet suffering eclipsing the devious times without number,
As the black sand clings and red and gold peppers
The conversation hot with injustice in a droning monotone,
Recognised and heard from Beirut to New Delhi as weird whimpers,
Belonging to ancient times, and acknowledged by those with good
    intentions.
Moony, hence the name, adding gall to the wound of Banjo Patterson.
Place of the galling moon, the gallstones of Henry Lawson
Seeks a little recognition in the signs of a verse akin to his own,
Veining the Ever-lastings, so pink and wonderous of my land.
But I have forgotten you, but I have deceived you,
But I have never wanted the petals to fall,
Scattered over the moonstones like random fancies.

(Stradbroke Island, December 1988)

THE SONG CIRCLE OF JACKY

Jacky him been sit listening to the wind;
Jacky him been walk listening to the wind;
Jacky him been sit talking to the wind;
Jacky him been walk following the wind.

Song One

Jacky's features worn and craggy,
The face of the cliff behind his place,
Worn and fissured with the care of his race,
Seeing them come and seeing them go,
Bodies bent or straight, weak or strong –
Seeing them go and wanting to follow,
First, he must fix his self and his self:
Jacky's not one to forget, remembering too much,
Remembers it all and wants to know more,
Wants to forget wages of flour, sugar and tea,
Wages of flour, sugar and tea, and women bought for a drink.

Jacky sits under the sun, feeling the warmth so good,
Feeling himself lying back, reclining with his head in his hands,
Reclining and thinking drowsily in the shade.
Peaceful his body, restless his mind,
Father tall and strong and fretful,
Circumcised into the Rain Dream, born from the Lizard,
Cast out at a little place, on a table in a shed,
Near a town, a whiteman's town, not too good or bad for Kooris.

Jacky lying back, body resting, mind, it roams,
Riding a wind, holding on and recalling –
His wife, a lissom girl with a tongue as quick as her wit.
Met her in some other place and took her back
To his shack, now a house, where she does what she does.
Of the Frog Dream mated with the Dog,
Woman rounded of breasts and thighs,
Rounded and a mother of two boys and girls.

Two boys, the eldest ran the store;
Followed the old ways and had been made a man;
Other still in school, beard beginning to show,
Just the other day copped for underage drinking.
Eldest daughter, sixteen married herself to a man
He did not like, one who wore suits and spoke with a lisp,
Collected a salary, now she was pregnant and lived in the town.

80 Mind restless, mind roaming this way and that,
    Daughter, a baby herself, now a mother too soon –
    Well, that was life, and when was the last time he had gone
    Hunting for a 'roo or even a cow, rabbits don't count,
    He thought as he lay, while the sun
    Made a run up the sky and fell over
    In a blazing circle of thunderclaps ripping the earth,
    And wrenching from the craggy cliff-face
    A boulder beginning to fall,
    Crashing down and rolling along to Jacky,
    Picking him up and taking him home to tea and scones.

Song Two

Many spirits make themselves known to him, known to him
As he sits, as he dreams in secret places, holes and creeks and hidden valleys,
As he sits in secret places, in holes and creeks and hidden valleys,
In forest clearings and dry desert gullys, in places lone and lonely.
In the night he walks to meet them, in the great heat he sees them;
In the black storm clouds and the dry dust winds he sits
Amid thunder and mirage, sits amid thunder and mirage and sees them.
Jacky walks when trees crash, Jacky walks when people huddle fearful;
Jacky is a doctor, Jacky sees what others do not wish to see.

He takes young man, he takes old man, makes them shiver in fright and fear;
He takes young man, he takes old man, makes them see his visions;
Makes them shiver in fright and fear, makes them suffer from the storm;
Makes them see their spirit maker, makes them leave him all alone,
While he finds his secret things, sacred objects of his trade:
Whispers to the magic wand, sings softly to the dilly bag,
Murmurs to the emu feathers, lights the fire with a word,
Brings the whirlwind to his feet, glides off to see the world:
Jacky Jacky, he no fool; Jacky Jacky, he kurdaitcha man!

Song Three

Joyful die young,
Sad live on:
Consensus and compromise,
Violence and fear.

Joyful die young,
Sad live on:
Injustice and hate,
Petty greeds and jealousies.
Youth seek relief in crime;
Old seek relief in perversion.

Old grow old,
Poor in lost opportunities,
Rich in lost souls:
All aimlessly wandering.

Joyful die young,
Sad live on:
Consensus and compromise,
Violence and fear.

Song Four

They march on Anzac Day morning,
Old and grey, weak and lame –
The only young, lost memories of
An aging, tortured, past Asian war,
Present with sudden tempers and strange births.
They march on Anzac Day morning –
The very young clanking with the weight
Of Grandad's medals swinging in rows,
Like colourful, beer-bottle tops.

They shout on Anzac Day afternoon,
Applauding a different kind of courage,
Of youthful victories and defeats,
Heavy with the aged wisdom of past days.

Anzio becomes equated with VFL Park,
Gallipoli with the slaughter of the 'Pies by the Demons',
Who in the raging last minutes of the battle
Went down, flying flags of victory in another defeat.

On Anzac Day evening, in hotel bars, aged warriors discuss
Old matches, old campaigns, old seasons and old wars:
Montgomery's strategy mingles with that of the latest Barassi,
Tobruk and how the Swans could not break through
The defence of the Steadfast Blues;
How the Bombers attacked again and again –
To be repelled by swarms of Hurricanes and Spitfires,
To be repulsed by the Bloody Mauler and the Terrible Twins,
Egged on by a crowd jangling medals of their past days
As they call for blood and guts, sacrifice and victory.
Jacky hears the last siren blending with the last trumpet
As he leaves the ground aching with victory and defeat.

Song Five

Ned Kelly, the Irishman,
Disliked the English,
For tyranny,
Carried on in the new country.

Left alone to do as he pleased,
He might have died just a farmer;
Left to law and legend,
He became a sort of hero,
Discussed by school girls and boys.

Life is not as absurd as reasoned,
Man is more than a useless passion
Strung up on the gallows tree,
Either as a hero or a crim –
Decide, to choose or not to choose?
Much like, to shave, or not to shave.

(*so all together now*)

Ned Kelly was a man,
Who rode through this land,
An' Irishman, brave and true –
Then the British hung him high,
So that his feet danced in the sky –
And Jacky says they did the same to –
Yagan, Melville Harry, Broger, Lory Jack,
Ellemara, Talboy, Merridio, Therramitchie,
And many, many, too many Jacky Jackies.

Song Six

Terribly distressing,
Whites go on and on,
Australians wrecking the land.
Aborigines pass a bottle,
Discuss relatives and strategy;
Whites go on and on and on
Without accepting our land.

Jacky, what feel for England?
Many come from there.
A social system,
Loves and hopes,
Men and women,
Stay-at-homes and runaways:
Another country just like –
India,
Cambodia,
Thailand,
Germany,
Or France,
No home.

Many come from there,
Elsewhere,
Go on being Australian.
Aborigines pass a bottle,
Sort out kinship groupings,
How Jacky fits as a relative;
Whites go on and on,
A people a long way from home.

Song Seven

In memory of Bob Marley, died 11 May 1981

Rastaman, 'e come Australia;
Rastaman, 'e come our land;
Rastaman, 'e see how they treat I,
See I and I, have no land, holes in the ground;
See I and I no land, only holes in ground:
An' 'e got pain in chest,
An' 'e feel it in breast.

Rastaman, 'e listen I and I;
Rastaman, 'e sing I and I;
Sing, Stand up for your rights,
Sing, Zion Land your own holy land.

Rastaman, 'e sing us out of fear;
But 'e see those holes in ground;
Sing the blame and sing the name;
Rastaman, 'e feel our pain:
A bullet in 'is chest,
A knife in 'is breast.

Now Rastaman, 'e track all over our country,
Drink our water, eat our 'roo, and taste our herb.
'E walk this way, 'e walk that way,
Fill those holes in the ground.

Faster 'e fill, faster they dig;
Faster 'e fill, faster they dig,
Turn into big rock to save one place,
Turn into big rock, sits there still –
Pain in head and pain in chest,
For I and I 'e die, for I and I 'e die,
Singin' out a song to protect the land.

Song Eight

They give Jacky rights,
Like the tiger snake gives rights to its prey;
They give Jacky rights,
Like the rifle sights on its target.
They give Jacky rights,
Like they give rights to the unborn baby,
Ripped from the womb by its unloving mother.

They give Jacky the right to die,
The right to consent to mining on his land.
They give Jacky the right to watch
His sacred dreaming place become a hole –
His soul dies, his ancestors cry;
His soul dies, his ancestors cry:
They give Jacky his rights –
A hole in the ground!

Justice for all, Jacky kneels and prays;
Justice for all, they dig holes in his earth;
Justice for all, they give him his rights –
A flagon of cheap wine to dull his pain,
And his woman has to sell herself for that.
Justice for all, they give him his rights –
A hole in the ground to hide his mistrust and fear.
What can Jacky do, but struggle on and on,
The spirits of his Dreaming keep him strong!

Song Nine

Long way from Nunkanbah –
Pestilential fetal phantasms.
Long way from Nunkanbah –
Baby, baby quite contrary
How do your phobias grow?
Long way from Nunkanbah,
Injustice, dead futureless hope.

Don't tell me about your miserable childhoods
Wraithlike boys and girls,
While our lives are sunless and landless,
While our lives are drank dry with hopeless future.

Don't declaim your anti-social ravings clad in suits,
While I study the latest figures numbring our dead babies.
Don't explain about your aching balls and tits,
While I hear of tourists creeping to photograph
Entwined 'coons' on a dry river bed they call home,
Right near where they took our rock and thought to keep it,
Though the yellow dog in warning, took a sacrifice.

Song Ten

Last Land Right's demo is over, is over,
The allies pack their bags and run,
Pack their bags, but black youth make a stand,
On Capital Hill, on Capital Hill,
Where the maggies squawk a fond hello,
And welcome to the site of the Magpie Dreaming.

People come and people stare,
Ignore any attempts at why we care,
But high flies the Black, Red and Gold,
High flies the Black, Red and Golden Sun.

People come and people stare,
Hardly exchange a word to the homeless youths,
Broke, but hopeful under the golden sun.
Sick of city slums, Redfern and Fitzroy,
Sick of pigs, blows and booze,
Sick of sadness, filled by hope –
Going to stay on till they get their rights,
Going to stay on till we get our rights,
While people come and people go,
Snapping shots at the city below.

Land Land Right's demo just over,
Allies pack their bags and run,
Run while Black Youths make their stand
On Capital Hill and talk of the Magpie Dreaming.
Now they are no longer there, no bags to pack,
But they have gone, gone away with Jacky and his kind,
And the magpies flutter their wings to Redfern and Fitzroy.

Song Eleven

Our demands you negotiate: we want our rights!
Our traditional land to be ours for ever.
Our sacred places ever sacred under our lawful keepers.
Our ancestors stood and fought: mark those places!
Our mission homes, where you put us: ours!
Our losses must be paid for: compensation
To those forced off their lands by alien hands,
Compensation to the lost and forsaken.
Pay, so that Australia may be made whole:
Pay, for old crimes never tried or justice passed.
Pay, part of the money you make from our land,
We never surrendered, or sold to you;
Pay with no conditions or political tricks;
Pay, negotiate the terms with us,
Free our land from blood debt,
And festering wounds of discontent.
Pay and free us from your welfare cheques,
And hat-in-hand and condition-laden grants.

Song Twelve

ay re amar ay re amar kacha

Jacky watches kitten, black as Rastafarian
Song condemning debris of history, evil Babylon;
Jacky watches unripe, leaping, scratching, kicking,
Rushing, whirling, staggering with apparent
Underlying steadying of ordered universe,
Marked out, insistent rhythm of African drums.

Oh old, oh over-ripe, oh rotten! –
Missing both incessant rhythm, broken rhythm;
Drum rhythm; burra rhythm; tam-tam rhythm
Sustaining universe, old but unworn time.
Oh old, oh cowardly, oh over-ripe – dying,
Forgetting leaping kitten of youthful age.
Ah green, ah unripe:
Guitar solo of unrhythmic shrieks screaming
Death black and white oppressors:
Fires birthing new world, green, holy!

Song Thirteen

Blank faces of a bored elite,
Hungup smiles of economic junky wiles,
The scramble of a research paper
Genuinely written for humanity.

Tired experiments done with tired hands:
Did the mind behind the fogged spectacles
Of his own boring mediocrity ever consider
That he too might make his mark in a bigger
World made up of something other than the economic whine
Of higher salaries, study leaves, pensions and superannuations?

Song Fourteen

It's strange how some people can laugh at rape;
It's strange how some people can laugh at murder,
Pain, stupidity, ignorance and last year's losers.
It's strange how laughter often is a grimace of contempt,
Directed at what we fear, hate, or want to mistrust.

Jacky walks down a street, the street all white;
Jacky sits in a show, the laughter all white
As a stabbing knife in thwarted mugging.
'I forget to take my twenty dollars and had to run;
But his blade outsped my legs by a few short inches.'

It's strange how people laugh at one another's hurtings;
It's strange how some people laugh at their own sadness,
While just wanting a shoulder to cry and be happy on;
But all the comfort they find is a laugh echoing,
Hollow and deep and sobbing with their loneliness.

Song Fifteen

It was day of multiple choices –
To get angry, to say 'no',
To say 'yes', to continue,
To go back, but ever forward.

It was just one of those days –
A no-no, yes-yes day,
Mediocre with multiple choices.

And so Jacky has arrived here along
With Polynesians talking of 'brothers'
And putting down the great white lies;
And so he has come here, has come here
Bringing a smile to exchange with chanting Maoris.

And what does it all mean, –
This strange place, this strange place
Along with the day of multiple choices:
The meaning is in the bringing,
What the morrow will bring to me.

Song Sixteen

A grasping at the sentimental, a boy and his dog;
Romantic tinges of the soul, Huck Finn and Sawyer;
The long sweep of the river floating with subservient friendly blacks;
A grasping at the heroic in thousands of clean towns;
The cowpoke's hat shades his bleak, watchful eyes,
Hiding his pain at never being clean and right,
Not even the feel of a kind hand, before he rides into the setting sun
Leaving the folks to meet a saviour, someday, sooner or never.
A grasping at the trivial, reaching for the moon –
To paper it over with aluminium ensquaring plastic and plastic:
A plastic man in a plastic suit on a plastic moon,
With 'Gee Whizz' sounds jerking the life from a stone.
America, Jacky saw your golden skin;
America, Jacky touched your shivering flesh;
He felt your anger quiver in your hates and loves,
And felt your bombs burn his peasant skin
While knowing the lily-white couldn't endure the sun
Even of California where snow is manufactured for a dollar.
America, Jacky has little to say to you,
He tries, but your strident voices shout him down
When he wanders along your tracks, an eight lane highway,
His blood splattering and streaming from coast to coast.

Song Seventeen

They call us terrorists, we – the terrified!
Soldiers came to our village, soldiers came to
Our jumbled low mud walls topped by palm fronds,
Soldiers came bouncing in shiny new jeeps, clutching
Shiny new rifles to take our shiny new school roofed with iron,
Thatched with our hopes, our despairs and future gains.

Now we have a shiny new police station;
Now we have shiny new police in shiny new uniforms;
Now we have army patrols and broken down walls;
Now we have shiny new planes, and have no homes;
Now we live in the hills – we, the terrified
Cower in the hills, and they call us terrorists
With our burnt out fields and working men's hands;
Now they call us terrorists – though we have only a single bullet
For our antique rifles – but the will to get more!

Song Eighteen

In 1914 I was young and creative:
Then I made my first attempt,
Tried bullets and bayonets,
And killed millions of my selves;
But not enough, I still survived.

I ached and pained:
Enclosed in hospitals,
I dreamt inventions,
And had to try again.

In the 30s, I used the aeroplane,
Followed it up with careful plans of gas ovens,
I bombed and shot, hacked and cut;
In the last explosion thousands died to add
To the millions dead; but I still survived!

To end my self, to end my selves,
I employed scientists and set them to work;
They discovered napalm and how it hurt;
Thousands suffered, yet I still survive,
Planning the final solution to my self, to my selves.

Song Nineteen

Underground – don't try to find us;
Underground – how we hurt, aching
For the best for all of us,
Suffering for the best for all of us.
Dried up tears in cheap hotel rooms,
Padded cells filled with misunderstanding:
We wanted the best for all of us, for all of us
While bullets flew and we cried and died.
Fewer and fewer, day by day we die, we die
In cheap hotel rooms and padded cells.
Ideals we were, we thought we were,
Now, you know where to find us.

Song Twenty

1

The shuffling drunk, the street derides,
His flaking face baffles the day.
God, staggers, sly in drunken rage.
A heavy fist, sodden and numb
Crashes, vibrating the parking meter,
All around the middle-class recoil.

The shabby line writhes to move,
In hunger twisted, bloodless veins,
Five dollars a quart to buy,
Then wine to rebuild the battered cells,
And food, the snaking line writhes still,
Voicing motherfucking threats of death.

Violence stumbles, shambles in bleary-blind,
To be kicked out on his scabby arse,
Voices mutter, whining for and against
An unfeeling flesh struggling with the warmth
Of wine, dirt and hopeless numb life,
Stranded from Folsom to San Quentin.

Man by shifting man the serpent glides
Hissing towards vegies and stew,
Stale cakes and tepid black coffee
Dark as the rooms vacant of souls
Long gone elsewhere to far suburbs,
Leaving Jacky alone with an aching stomach-self.

2

No rent, this time is over,
This weary hotel room rest.
Old newspapers scattered over the floor,
Stained sheets flecked with tobacco flakes,
A broken wardrobe, crumbled twisted hangers,
A bag, a stuffed snout on the dirty floor,
A few magazines left with the yellow wash-basin,
A chest of drawers filled with empty bottles and cans.

No hope – traffic roars through the window
Flashing with a red and green store sign.
No hope – a radio stutters through the open door,
The speckled mirror shows no hope.
No hope – Jacky humps his bag and treads away:
Hope – two dollar key deposit.

3

Written out in triplicate,
Survival in capitalist gloom,
IDed and imprinted in wax:
Too bad, a rest and out to try again.

In the night time light, the bars are singing,
Sung by a fiftyish woman in high white boots.
Grey hairs streaks rays into a whisky bottle:
What'll happen when she leaves?

In the Salvo centre, old boys rest
In anger, sober to earn a dime or two;
Then, break out, drink is death for life:
Pious souls wait, yet Jesus doesn't speak.

In the night time light, the band is swinging,
The drummer lurches into the hands of a cop:
'Leave me alone, I sing my cowboy songs.'
A snarl: 'Who wrecked the telephone?'

In the Salvo centre, quiet men seethe,
Seek fights in fitful moody growls:
'Get away, I'm off to have a drink.
Jesus saves – I hear it every day.'

Song Twenty-One

A bottle of wine, a warm, warm thrill.
Old men sitting, a seven-inch screen flickering
With all the signs of life gone dry with violence.
Jacky's seen the best minds lost to the TV set.
Thank God, I've got my screen to keep me company,
Together with a bottle of red and a cigarette
I'm happy, and I don't even feel a need.
The radio keeps on along, a pulsing disco beat
Of keep it up and on lest one day you awake
One day to shriek: My God, what's wrong –
No sights of yesterday's news swirling on the tube;
No sounds of the current tune rattling around the speaker;
My God, even the empty bottle is filled with loneliness.

Song Twenty-Two

The road is barred by temples and churches,
My Lord, Jacky hears your call and tries to run:
Prophets and gurus trip his feet and shout:
Your voice is lost in the din of ceaseless babble.
His soles are sore, his knees bare and bloody,
He limps on – but his desire for unity
Dies in a host of faiths screaming TRUTH.
At last, the door of love – bearing too many locks:
Krishna and Allah, Jesus and Kali, Mother and Father:
Poor Jacky sitting and crying in regret and frustration.

Song Twenty-Three

1

I know that I am –
No jargon, please –
I know that I am,
Water and earth
Mixed with a little wine.

Don't tell me who I am:
A child cries in me too often;
My mouth curves too often
In sadness these days.

I know that I am
Like a lonely child,
Locked in a black closet,
Huddled in the darkest, scariest corner.

Don't tell me who I am –
A deserted hotel room,
A sink in one corner,
A wardrobe, bed and chair:
No poetry, only a Rolling Stone
Opened at random notes.

2

If you want me, try your jails,
In solitude, a bible for my love.

If you want me, walk along a street
Holding in each dark doorway,
Nothing, but your middle-class do-gooder fear;
Then stop, look down, right down –
An empty bottle, a sprawled black body,
Pink streaming urine stinking of your wine.

104   If you want me, follow the screaming siren
Rushing pigs to crush our anger –
Brother against brother 'till they come
And hustle away the debris of our hope.

If you want me, try your grassless parks,
In solitude, old men drinking life away.

Song Twenty-Four

Clinging a little monkey to its mother ape,
Jacky clutches what is unreal as the past,
You sweet love, while he waits
For a new idea to grab all his mind.

Really, you took his mind as you took his body,
Taking all, refusing to be denied, anger calling,
Liberating while tying; acquiescent heat rising,
Panting for a single thrust to bring blood spurting.

Sky-walker, you rose on early morning mist,
Sub-zero cold, a sunless ground your landing field,
Though you left in summer clothing of tropic heat.
Yes, you rose and fled sunskinned girl,
Taking all that you needed to drift as a cloud.

Song Twenty-Five

Sun-patches scar the adult mind:
Black of skin; mother's warning:
Stay out of shadows, try to appear white,
Don't show the darkness,
Ever-present as your Aboriginality.
In that darkness father watching, waiting,
Lovingly as his son another drink taking –
Forget it, let it be!
Old stories lost in slimy time,
Learn to accept the father saves a child,
Fluttering with falling wings from heights non-attained.

Song Twenty-Six

This hooked throwing-stick of peninsular land,
Bunjil fashioned it.
With beak and claw he scored the earth,
The waters rose,
To enclose the shape,
For Eaglehawk to see
As he flew high
Scattering,
To drift down upon the land,
The seedlings of the Bunurong,
To grow from earth as bird from nest.

Song Twenty-Seven

A youthman was found hanging in his cell
On Nadoc day when everywhere the Aborigines
Were dancing, everywhere the Aborigines were marching.
'They're just like us,' was the quaint refrain,
'They like balls and footy and songs and beer':
They ignored our call for Landrights!

On Nadoc day a youthman strangled in a cell:
Who killed him; who were his murderers?
'Not I,' said the cop, 'I only took him in.'
'Not I,' said the town, 'I never spoke his name,
It's no fault of mine that he had to die –
We treat them as we would our own,
There's no racism in our town.'

On Nadoc day a youthman died while his people
Camped nearby trying to recover stolen land.
They daubed the town with Truth and raised high
The Red and Black and Gold:
The red was his blood;
The black his skin;
The gold his cause as bright as sun:
We want our land and there is no turning back!

Song Twenty-Eight

On the twentieth anniversary of Mao Tse-tung's death
The central Committee of the CPC
Decreed that his objectives had been reached
And forthwith sold China to GMA,
Before retiring to a geriatrics' home in Florida
Which they owned, livestock and commune.

GMA at a special stockholders' meeting
Announced in a 1000 page press release,
Summarising the gains and future prospects of the firm,
That they were world-winners in the capitalist stakes,
With over a billion employees, each paying a rent
Of a dollar a day for land on which to work.

Meanwhile not to be left out, the ALLP
Surveying world events with socialising eyes,
Behind liberal spectacles lightly dusted with country earth,
Declared for the sale, lock, stock and Aborigines,
Of Australia to GMH in the interests
Of all round prosperity plus the curbing of inflation,
And the paying of an army of anti-terrorist squads
Armed to the teeth to fight an opposition yet to appear.
The bill was presented and passed into act without a murmur,
The chip had long gone to an ALLP grave,
And it was in the middle of the footy season.
What followed next was GMA acquiring England,
France and all the rest in co-operation with USSR Incorporated.

Song Twenty-Nine

All the passionate young men,
Never having passed the manhood tests,
Have become old women sitting quietly
In fancy new houses in Canberra town,
Melbourne, Sydney, Adelaide and Perth.

Jacky-Jacky may drink plonk;
Jacky-Jacky may be old;
But 'e see all with wisdom eye,
Jacky-Jacky 'e kurdaitja man.

All the young'uns grown flabby
In white fellows' ways
Sit in offices on fat salary chairs,
Waiting for their superannuation couches,
While sending their gins to modelling schools
Where they learn how to hide their Koori legs.

Jacky-Jacky may be poor;
Jacky-Jacky may be blind;
But 'e kurdaitja man,
Curse them all with wisdom eye.

All the young'uns have grown sad
Fitting into white fellows' suits and ties,
Sitting all bored in office, house and town –
Remember, remember, there were certain families;
Remember, remember, your reservation home,
And certain houses and certain families,
And don't play rules and regulations –
Now we sit in Canberra town,
Drinking whisky and being neat,
Air conditioned against the heat.

Jacky-Jacky may be drunk;
Jacky-Jacky, they think 'e fool;
But 'e has wisdom eye,
Jacky-Jacky 'e kurdaitja man.

Song Thirty

'Mummy, mummy,
What's a Naboriginal?
One came to talk to us today –
What's a Nunkanbah?
Told us Captain Cook was bad,
Only came to steal this land –
Mummy, what's a Nembaluk?
Said that we had spoilt the ground,
Said that time would condemn us for our crime –
Mummy, do you know about the Unguru?
Said it was a great big snake;
Said it struck when it was hurt;
Said that it was hurting now –
Mummy, I'm too scared to cry,
I don't want our land to die.'
Jacky smiles, he's getting through.

Song Thirty-One

Let her rest; let her rest;
Too long she roamed; too long she roamed;
Let her rest, now that we have laid her down.

She lived; she lived; she watched her people die;
She lived; she lived; she felt her dead ones cry.
In grief she left her place, she left her place
To wander over the land, over the land to still her grief –
Her people's grief; her people's death.
She walked, she talked, she felt the scorn
Of alien eyes, of her people's tongues:
What could she do? She watched her people die,
While flattery touched her body and led her steps,
Marked her tracks to island exile, to island exile,
Marked her tracks to killing far away,
Far from home and then to island prison.
Her name was changed as she felt the fear,
The fear as the last of her menfolk died,
Far from home and island exile.
His body was raped and his balls were stolen;
His body was raped and they stole his balls;
Trugernanna felt the shame, felt his body's pain;
Felt the shame, felt all over his body's pain,
And wished to be laid to rest in the sea, in the sea,
Or a hillside slope, a far hillside,
Far from them with their callous minds and pitchfork lies.

And then she left, and then she died, no lying down,
No rest, they seized her bones, no rest, no rest,
A museum displayed her bones, a museum stored her bones,
No rest, no rest, her ghost it roamed, her ghost it cried,
And the black folk saw and heard her cries,
They fought to give her a grave, to give her a grave,
Far from those with callous minds and pitchfork lies.

Now let her rest; now let her rest;
Too long she roamed; too long she cried;
Now let her rest; now that we have laid her down;
Now that Jacky and his kind have laid her down.

Song Thirty-Two

Sweeping sadness of Balayang: Batman one with a problem;
Sweeping sadness of Balayang: miserable, upset,
Mean and bad, hanging there upside down.

Sadness of Balayang, sadness of Balayang: sadness, sadness.
Wife is dead: sadness, sadness. No woman, sad!
No woman to grow his vegetables, gather and cook them:
No woman, no woman, no woman's work,
Balayang is sexist, will waste away: no woman's work!

Yearning Balayang, track his steps to a camp,
The camp of his mother-in-law, his mother-in-law.
Wrong to speak to her, standing there dumb:
Her husband long dead; his wife just dead.
Woman no meat, man no vegetables: both are sexist:
No man's work!
No woman's work!

Man may find a way, but faster woman,
Left at his tent a basket of fruit,
Left them there without a care,
Knew that later she would find,
Kangaroo or possums in her camp.

But man needs more than chips with his steak,
Aching Balayang: old woman spied the reason.
Sung a song of power, walked and walked,
Walked towards a thickish log,
Struck it with her digging stick – crack!

Quivered and gaped out two young ladies,
Nimble and nice enough to accept her words:
Went laughing in mirth, went swimming in water,
Kicking with legs and splashing with hands:
Balayang was aroused and came.

Creeping through forest, creeping through bush,
Creeping ever nearer to trespassers on his land;
Standing up, fitting the spear to his thrower, seeing them;
Relaxing and smiling, accepting their cheeky words:
'Grandfather?' they giggled at him,
'Father, No! Well, brother then –
No, what then, but husband,' they shouted in glee,
Rushing him off and Balayang was husband.

Song Thirty-Three

Land sacred,
Lifegiving earth,
Not deathgiving dirt:
Spirits forced to roam,
Seek a new refuge in Truth.

Many find it – in death!
Jacky says: 'Machines come,
Put an end to our hopes,
Bitter truth rules here:
Earth once supporting life;
Earth, now providing graves.
Hidden, unlike the trees
In which once we hung
As our flesh rotted,
To free our spirits
From the haunted living.'

Song Thirty-Four

Long ago, his skin itches as men enter his pores
And run their fingers lightly along his walls,
Or scratch faintly diagrammatic lines.
From then on they touch Jacky in other ways:
The Wandjina eat themselves through his skin to become his bones.
White, yellow-haloed figures with gapped eyes
Searching for the tribal dead and the touching fingers
Of the living marking out the living.
In other places his skin is dotted, tapped and corroded by shapes;
Even the wraithlike Mimi emerge from between his cells
To line a rock with stick-like figures of grace
Which men might copy or trace with wondering nails.
The dancing Kwinkin quiver across his skin,
A hand is stencilled and a thylacine sketched.
Jacky's flesh shivers with thousands of tracks and figures and signs –
To be followed by strange horrific shapes,
Stranger men with stranger weapons,
To be etched and kept for all to see
That life is ever-moving, changing across his skin.

Song Thirty-Five

Forward our generation:
The next generation shall be heavy.
Jacky went with outstretched hand,
Armed only with a plea for justice –
What did they give him, give him?
Nothing, nothing, nothing but pain,
Drunkenness, despair and false promises.
Forward our generation:
The next generation shall be heavy!
There are no more 'nos';
No more 'pleases' – only 'thankyous'.
Our generation forward,
The next generation is heavy,
The tree has a mighty root,
The branches are strong
And flower this spring.

CALCUTTA
DREAMING

Travelling

With a friend to the airport,
Overflowing with rowdy Aussies,
Floating on stale beer vapours –
The jumbo is as late
As you would expect
The slowness of an elephant to be.
Waiting in the howdah of the airport;
Waiting in a sterile bitterness
Of an absence of travel drowned
In the odour of beer stained like piss.
A round of the dutiful desirable shops
Aiming to fulfil needs at the cheapest prices,
Then a sitting and a looking at less durable objects,
People, encased feet, heads, breasts and chests,
No similes, let alone metaphors.
Restless waiting in the restless eyes of a woman,
At last to enter a metal tube, entrailed,
Taken up to be digested,
And excreted as waste at Bombay.

An Offering

To Dr Atindra Mojumdar, my Bengali Teacher

O Bengal when I think of you,
I fall into images of Calcutta,
Where the tiger snarls lashing its tail,
Stalking the dawn-jungle streets for countless victims
Of their own distress, hunger seeking a full world.
O Calcutta, cities reek pollution of the spirit,
Souls become corpses of zombies there
Away from their village-homes amid the green
Of a great river delta silted in sorrow,
Divorced from the earth in chaos.
Find a place and sit dreaming of the coolness beneath;
Find a piece of ground and sit, letting the cooling
Thoughts of your Ganga Dreaming purify your mind.

Calcutta Dreaming

Calcutta dreaming, a glowing bride in red and gold,
Going to meet her husband with a lakh and a motor bike,
Perhaps she shall find love, dreaming love in Calcutta,
Dreaming love in rough male voices, the lark of a
Soaring female voice answering back in arabesques.

Calcutta dreaming nightmares in moody, violent sobs,
Of club-swinging cops moving things to the right,
Separating parties and possibilities, red against the tricolour,
The hard steel of hammer and sickle against the idealistic spinning wheel.

Calcutta dreaming dreams beside the Ganges,
How can I remember the Zion land of Ashoka times,
When strangers came to divide my land,
And sell it piece by piece to other strangers?
Calcutta dreaming dreams beside the Ganges,
Many exiles dream dreams in you.

Calcutta dreaming a past of dreams,
In young men aching dreams of the future –
Nightmares in the reality of senseless killings:
Now the TV dreams idle dreams for the idle,
Still an old man works his life away at seventy,
Dreaming dreams of an early retirement in death.

Calcutta dream broad avenue dreams,
In the narrow streets of endless traffic jams,
Jumbled images mixed in a Freudian confusion,
Of stumbling symbols reaching out a hand to feel a cow,
Saluting its forehead as it leaves for petrol free air:
The sky rains black pollution safe from holiness.

Calcutta, my dreaming mingles with your dreaming;
Your lanes and roads are my veins and arteries;
My heart is the rhythm-beats of your festivals;
My thoughts are the dances of your fickle moods;

My voice multiplies to become all your voices;
Exhausted, I am the immigrant workers lying in your dust.

Calcutta, my tears flow through your pipes to ease your thirst;
Calcutta, my blood is the wine intoxicating too many of your children;
Calcutta, my dreaming is so entwined with your dreaming,
That at times I feel myself sprawling beside the Ganges,
Loving my being in a multitude of sighs and passionate declarations,
Seeking to re-create your loveliness in a thousand kisses of a brilliant sprir
Softened by the cooling breezes of our age-old passion.

Calcutta in the Evening

On the verandah, I stand thinking of my love:
Against a dark wall, the black shape of a palm bends,
Countless voices drone the tamboura of the city,
    Above weaves the sitar of a poet.
To my right a baby cries, to my left a mother sighs,
Before me the husband shouts, and Grandfather mutters
    While I stand thinking of my love
In the evening raga uniting in a sudden quietness:
The palm sways as supple as her body,
And the flute of my sigh adds its magic
    To Calcutta in the evening.

Carla, Do Not Forget Calcutta

Do not forget Calcutta,
She, the withered goddess,
Has known too many lovers,
Now she lies sunk in dreams.

Do not forget Calcutta:
Many jewels gleam from unfinished settings,
Her passions have mellowed with age:
She stirs, then huddles again in sleep.

Do not forget Calcutta,
Her dreams colour the poetry of the morning;
A golden sun struggles to shimmer through her mists,
And her children fling off their nightmares,
Suddenly glimpsing her as she was and will be.

Harijan

Naming us the children of God,
Refusing us paradise,
Exiling us from the kingdom,
Oppressed by those who fear our touch,
Afraid to touch the children of God.
Murdering us – our blood and guts fertilise this land;
Raping our women – their tears and saliva are our sacrifice:
God will give us our promised land,
Earned by our sweat and the labours of our hands,
Our paradise created by our own efforts.

No more will our touch pollute – no more, no more;
No longer will they fear our touch – our touch no longer;
No more in fear of our lives – less than dust, in fear of our lives;
Free and equal, free and equal; our land our land, our land our land.

Our exile is over,
United we stand
With wrath, with humanity
Having earned our love.
We, the children of God,
That great man named us,
Going out to free a nation
In which we remain slaves,
Now, no more, no more,
Mahatmaji, no more!

Devi

She lived near that famous house in Calcutta,
Where bombs were made in troublesome times;
Where youths came and went armed up
To explode the city with thunderous change.
Then were the times for an artist to seize and capture;
Mouths strained in the primal agony of hunger and revolt;
The old world struggling to give birth to the new;
Aborted by army knives in a cold rage of ownership,
And political rhetoric fleeing the pangs of birth.
Devi captured the pregnancy and the abortion;
Then fled into interior decorating
When the times remained with the old
People survived and the government was kinder,
After they had killed the father of a fertilised womb.
Now she worms into her culture
Where women have long eyes reaching to their ears,
And revolution is part of a romanticised near-past,
When she lived near that famous bomb factory,
Where youths came and went armed up,
To explode the town with thunderous reaction.

Men

Once we were men, men,
Now our bodies as slight, as slight
As the weakest of your women.
Talk to us and we'll say,
You get more food in your prisons.
Malnutrition stalks us all,
Poor bodies, at birth they ceased to grow;
Poor bodies, no fat around the bones,
No calcium in the thighs,
Kick us and we'll break,
Like the dolls destroyed by your children.
It is too late for us; too late even for our babies,
We'll say 'Yes' to every question you demand an answer,
We have the need and you can cave in our ribcage with a blow.
God do not forsake us, Kalima preserve us,
Our lives are less than the dust we stumble over,
Less than the hopes of that man who gave us hope,
And the words to declare that when we die you die:
The survivors fear nothing you can bring against them.

Sold and Delivered

I sold myself for a few pieces of silver,
The acid of my soul
Turned the metal bitter black.
I sold myself to thee,
I was hungry and all that I needed
Was a handful or two of rice:
It gave me the strength to hate, to know
That a man cannot sell himself.
Now I stand straight before you,
Though my wife and children clutch my ankles,
I stand straight before you
Demanding my inheritance
Which is mine by right.
I stand straight before you
And refuse to beg;
Give me my inheritance,
And I shall set you free;
Refuse, you refuse,
You shall pay the penalty!

1

Come brothers, come together,
Seek out the way to prosperity;
Let us plough and trade and work with our hands,
Let us become educated, then we shall rise anew.

2

Shaking off sleep and rubbing their eyes,
Everywhere, people are rising –
Why, unconscious like logs and stones?
Everywhere, the light of knowledge is dawning –
Everywhere, your snores loudly fill your darkness.
Everywhere, people are advancing,
You alone lie still.
Everywhere, people racing ahead,
You not even crawling a few inches.
Everywhere, people ascending to the skies –
How long shall you stay down
When even those below have passed you?
They trample upon us – let us arise!
How many of us have light and learning:
What do we do for the good of all?
Our educated are content only to fill the belly;
How sad, how sad they are stuffing their little belly,
Like the crow, the fox and the bear.
You were born a human, higher than these;
But all you care about is self:
No good for your land and your people!
Listen to me, you Hos,
Get up and work for all;
Get up, struggle for people and country.
O brothers, the times have changed, changed,
No more do the drums pound in love and joy –
Now the rhythm flows for the good of all.

Don't toss your head in the dance;

Don't drink bottle after bottle,
Then reach for the larger flagon and cask
For more and more – no thought for your country!
Drunkards, get to your feet and untie yourselves,
Drive off evil customs and join with the world.
Listen, listen, to what I have to say:
Old ways linger in you though your body be changed.
Outdoing the English in cutting and combing the hair,
In your clothing and use of scent you mock the Bengalis,
But you are ignorant and scentless like the Polash flower.

3

In the garden, the eye-entrancing rose
In full bloom, spreads its fragrance.
It opens and beams bright for a time,
Then withers away to dry flakes.
How sad – one day to bloom, the next to fade;
But though those petals die, a treasure remains,
Deogam, the poet made this song
In praise of the treasure left behind
After the fading, after the colour decaying
Until all beauty is traceless –
Still the breeze touching that dryness
Spreads sweet perfume everywhere.
This is your fate, O mankind,
Your loveliness shall shine bright only for a day,
Even though you frequent physicians death will come
And leave you withered, dead petals on a broken stem.
What use are beauty and youth – they arrive and go:
Do good deeds in this world and your name
Endures and emits the fragrance of the rose.

4

At sunrise, the sunbeams are red,
And it's easy to get food and drink,
Young life drifts on pleasantly
Without storms and cares:
Happily you sit in the shade of your parents.

134   At noon, the easy sunbeam turns hard,
You have to work for your food and drink,
Days are planned and the easy drifting is no more:
Life does not glide, but lurches from fear to distress.

Take care then, even in the rising sun
Be prepared for strife and the noon heat,
Set your face and struggle against your fears,
Or they will overcome you:
Work hard and make open the road before you.

Love Song

I have no need of love songs,
Rani is my wife,
She works beside me in the fields,
She is black but comely:
That is what they say.

Rani is my life,
Young and lithesome,
Strong to plant the paddy,
She might have borne me sons,
But she was black and comely:
At least that is what they said.

Rani was my wife,
They took her away one day,
I found her naked in the field,
Black but ugly,
Her terrified mouth stuffed with dirt.

Now I sing my love song,
How long, My Lord, how long?
Rani was my wife,
Now I sit beside the roadside,
Singing: Rani, my life is gone.

Purnima

With love-pressed tears,
The trains dim as they go by:
I try to speak, but what to say?
I turn only to fall into your eyes,
And I long to see you
In every single blade of rice in every field;
And I long to fall a thousand times,
Drowning in those two dark lakes.
Govinda dances on a worldly wave,
And who is the willing slave of that black Krishna?
Moon shines on the soft, dark earth;
Earth shines on the stained whiteness of the moon,
And our bodies reflect both united in our love.

Renunciation

Such is the pain caused by your careless eyes,
That I feel like a man drowning in a dark lake.
When I think of you such is the sadness,
That I feel that I have no home.
I shall become a sanyasi,
And wander through the forests of your hair.
I shall become a sanyasi,
And do penance to gain your beauty.

What is life without you? –
My heart is restless and my mind seeks
The relief of strange pastures of sweet-smelling herbs.
I will become a sanyasi,
And journey, worshipping each and every footfall
Of your blushing feet gracing the earth.
I will become a sanyasi,
And seek union in your divinity.

FRINGE POEMS

All Life Long

When I was born Spaniard was killing Spaniard;
When a baby, Hitler was launching his legions
To build a new world carpeted with corpses.
My tiny lungs filled with poison gas;
My little body was flung into the furnace:
Too thin to make soap, it made fertiliser.
When a child, they were fighting to save Korea,
White men killing other folk as they always had.
Growing older in massacres and mutilated bodies;
Everywhere flickering the fires of wartime suffering:
India against Pakistan, Israel against Arabia;
The joys of napalming peasants in far Vietnam,
Turning as sour as the stench of burning flesh.
Buddhists against terror and the fires of a blazing body –
I felt the agony as a man and my heart remained intact,
A scorched lump of flesh, an offering towards peace,
While they fight on ridding the world of isms and schisms,
In the murder of countless millions of feeling people
Longing for something a little better to leave to their children.

I Am

I am the blonde SS man
Strong, but subservient to the doctrine
Of a purity beyond human pain;
I am the shadow slinking in your mind,
So dark, so scary –
But created by you:
Once you killed us, once you enslaved us,
In a hatred beyond warm flesh and blood.
I am the sickness in your soul,
The seeking beyond remorse;
But you are guilty in your worship of strange unclean things,
While our hard hearts still can remain warm enough to bleed,
Living on and loving the womb which gave us the life to birth.

Song

Tonight I saw the stars falling,
Last night I felt the red Mars calling
Imploring me to rise to the sun
And be free of the scum-filled
Days of my childhood life.

Tonight I see the stars falling
To earth in scattered diamonds of exploding
Facets of light soaring out in rays
Of glistening sentience.

O my mind-filled mood of fire-freeing
From the mire of long-lost habits
That still entrap:
And completely wrap and rap –
Rap, rap at my mind-door seeking
An entrance, seeking an exit to free
Me completely from right and wrong
That is mightily strong and endures
Long – until the life-force fails,
And I sail way, way up there.

Last night, I saw the stars falling,
Tonight, I feel the red Mars calling
Imploring me to rise to the sun:
And up and up I soar, free
To where the Father waits for me.

Art

Taking art into their lives,
Thinking it gave beauty,
Taking art into their lives:
Oh, African beauty,
Our tracks crisscross,
Meet, part, cross again,
Small in the setting sun,
Large in the rising moon,
Oh, African beauty,
I recognise your tracks
Beside the wading pool,
Hesitating at my feet imprinted
Beside the wading pool.
Oh, African beauty,
I follow your tracks
A little way beyond,
Then lapsing into a certain forgetfulness,
Wander off – to meet again your tracks,
At the opera house, at the war monument,
At nightclubs faceless with white flesh.
Now our tracks stagger without firmness;
Now they meander seemingly without purpose,
Ever-seeking unconsciously for what makes our world entire.

Men's Business

Around camp at sunset,
Odd word
Exchanges a thought,
Single word,
Thick with meanings.

Moon rises,
Marking sky
With time,
Time go,
Go!
Others squat
Urgent unheard meanings;
Locked actions,
Swift, sharp, whole
In the new being,
Emerging,
Damp moonlight,
Dark dampness,
Flowing wounds of adulthood.

There Is Love

There is love around the bend,
Where the forked lightning splits;
There is love around the bend,
Where the kangaroo inclines in obeisance;
Where men sit intent in their thoughts,
Thinking while the women's ceremony unfolds
Beyond their gaze – in their thoughts,
Though beyond their thoughts, beyond their vision.

There is love around the bend,
Lost in the haze of a smoothed escarpment;
There is love, intense and straight,
Where the women conduct their ceremonies,
Beyond the vision of men, beyond their thoughts,
Where the earth turns into female ground,
Where the grains of dust cling and cling;
There is love there – forces of attraction,
Beyond where the men sit intent in their thoughts.

Granny Mary came walking down our way,
Her steps were slow, but her feet was strong;
Granny Mary came walking all down our way,
Pointing out the things that we had lost.
We took her in and gave her a feed,
Some damper to keep her strength up strong.
Granny Mary, she told us what it was all about,
Told us about the times she had lived,
Said she had seen the men shot down,
Given flour, sugar and tea,
Just to keep their hands up strong,
Working for the boss, working for the bossman,
Till he was told that he had to pay us wages,
Then it was, he chased us to this town.
Granny Mary, she worked in the bighouse,
Cooked and scrubbed for the Gubbas,
And what she got for her wage,
She cried when she told us About That!

Granny Mary came walking out of a bright sunny day,
Came to us and told us about the sins we didn't commit,
Told us of the blight over the land and how it was sick,
She raised her fist, it was black and strong
As she told us, if you think you're Gubbas,
Go to the front of the pub and not the back.
Granny Mary came walking up to us one day,
I sat and listened and said: 'What did you get?'
And she answered back: 'Sweet fuckall!'

What happened to me and Bobby?
Bobby got jugged in Derby,
Went to jail for a year or so,
Now he walks the streets of Perth alone,
Holding out his hand for a coin
To make up a bottle or few.
Me, I ended up Broome way,
Loving creeps for a cent or two,
One day I'll take to the road again,
And fuck my way down south to you.
What is life, it's feeling blue,
And longing for that Bobby McGee,
Drinking down that plonk in Perth,
Strumming a chord on his old guitar,
For a drink to drown his sorrows,
Memories of a brown girl who gave him nothing,
But a talking he didn't listen to.

The NAC Song

Relyin' on the gub'ment for our pay,
Compensation's 'ard to get,
Relyin' on the gub'ment.
Some people get a fat salary.
What they do, Christ, I do know,
Got our members, got to keep on pushin' for our rights;
Got our members, got to keep 'em pushin' for our rights,
Give 'em the power to use their skills where it counts,
Ain't no use to just have them stuck way out in the bush.
Me an' me mates, we voted for Alec;
Me an' me mates, we voted for Merle,
They knew us an' talked our lingo,
Best to have someone there who knows your mind.
Fightin's not enough when you ain't got the skills,
A car's fine as long as you can drive it on the job.
Some people's puttin' down the NAC,
Seems like once they fought for it one time,
Just remember we voted for Merle and Alec,
We even hear their feet runnin' about in circles
In that gub'ment town called Canberra,
Where some folks wear suits and ties and call us kin.

Under An Aboriginal Tree

Under an Aboriginal tree,
Scrawny and willowy
Just like me, naturally,
I thought –
Where do those thick fellows come from?

Next to a kangaroo –
Ever tried getting close
To one of those fellows? –
You have to look like a brother,
I thought:
This one'll taste good in the cooking pot.

Next to my white brother –
I thought: Brother?
Got legs and arms
And things like that –
Been out of the sun though –
And my brother turned to me,
Said: 'You want Australia.'
And I said: 'Right on, Jack,'
And walked away.
If they think like that,
We'll take back Australia,
And send 'em all back home.

Country Dog in the City

Earth flat, hard, petrified clinging smells,
Clicking of my nails on the black harness of thought,
Grass softens the impact of my scent seeking out
Titbits of what I used to know beneath the cloth of passersby,
Stranger smells of piss, pools of feeling overcome by shit.
Country dog in the city, sights and scenes and worthless sighs
For a countryside flowing with the high tips of reaching beyond,
Slow and sure, green or dry in the overtaking seasons,
Seeds of life drag at my coat as I wander the mirage of ground water,
Stopping to take a long drink of reality before shaking it off.
Country dog in the city, snuffling up and sneezing out,
The griminess of the day coated with a denial of nature's needs,
The awful boredom of the flatness of the floor-smelling fluff;
The awful boredom of minds processed and divided into tins,
Scentless with the sterility of another day gone into nightmares,
Flecked with the gentle dreams of another time of scents and feelings,
Country dog in the city, endure, it was this life or a country bullet.

City Suburban Lines

Their roads are straight;
Their streets are straight;
Their fences are straight;
Straight are the bricks
Of their walls,
As straight as the lines
Of their vehicle-minds,
Rushing in straight thoughts
To straight feelings.

Unholy is their straightness;
Their religion is straight,
Bound between straight
Lines in a book whose prose
Has been straightened,
And made to move along
The straightness of their lives.

Straight are the pictures on their walls;
Straight, ensquaring lines unfeelingly straight
With moods straight from the strayed lines
Of tendered gardens straight with the stems
Of flowers modified into straightness.

Straight is the world they have fashioned;
Straight are the walls of their imprisoning cells;
Straight are the lives we are forced to endure:
Born between straight lines;
Dying between straight lines;
Laid to rest between straight lines,
Buried in rows as straight as supermarket goods:
Our heaven will be straight lines;
Our hell will be all curved lines,
Unable to fit the straightness of our souls.

Hide and Seek

Hidden in hidden rooms,
Afraid to face
A glimmer of truth,
Wives and kids
Hardly speaking a word,
Except to demand.
Speak, reply, mumble.
Once men were mythologies;
Once spears were clutched;
Once our words ran together,
In complex sentences of intent;
Now we have become monosyllables,
Lonely in straight streets,
As long as the sentences
We once formed
From our initiation marks,
Cut deeply into our living flesh,
By masters of our languages.

Lord Help Us

Lord help us, poor boong tasted the wine,
And forgot his culture, forgot his dancing feet.
Poor Jacky Jacky forgot his corroborees;
Teach us again the ceremonies, Oh Lord,
Teach us the way back, the way forward;
Mark out the land anew, mark out the land a'old,
Bring together our brothers and sisters,
Mothers, fathers, aunts and uncles,
Terrible old grandmothers and grandfathers,
Old King Billys and Willys, Jackys and Marys,
Now lost as the land, lost in the land,
All lost as Jacky Jacky who tasted the wine,
And forgot his culture, forgot his corroborees.

Sing sadness, sing sadness over our land;
Sing sadness, sing sadness throughout our land;
We have failed ourselves, sing sadness.
Poor Jacky Jacky tasted the wine,
And forgot his culture, his ceremonies,
Sing sadness, sing sadness, English culture,
Sing sadness, a Dreaming from a faraway land,
Where the sun does not take revenge, revenging
Itself on white flesh bared in a black land;
Revenging itself on a white culture reshaping our land.

Watch Your Step

Walking down the street at midnight,
Feeling strong and free in your newest of gear,
Car slowing to follow, command: 'Get in!'
Down to the station,
Down with your strength,
Strong you were in your newest of gear,
And a belt or two beneath your pants,
Looking black and boong to them.
Lips tighten and you want to be free,
Fist in the belly don't leave no scars,
Excepting in your mind,
Warned: they don't take no shit,
From the likes of you in your newest of gear,
Leaving no marks, your belly bleeding inside.
A boong ain't got no rights in this flaming world,
Your newest of gear, it don't make no change,
Just take to drink, and it's 'Jacky, you've had too much.'
Off to jail for a day sober or two,
Long lost your pride along with your gear,
Living is surviving for evermore.

Goomee

In clarity, my mind watches,
Watches the lurching of my drunken body;
In drunkenness, clear and entire,
My mind watches, clear and entire
My perilous wanderings through a strange world,
Filled with sudden frights – no dreams
I see as I lurch, lurch and feel:
Their conquering has lost them their hidden eyes;
Their conquering has meant their blindness
To a tree mating with the sky.
My staggering steps make few tracks,
Undecipherable, they cannot follow
My anger, their hidden eyes are blind,
In their blindness they have lost me,
In my drunkenness have I lost me?

On the Outskirts

On the outskirts of your eyevision,
On the outskirts of your earhearing,
On the outskirts of your brainthinking,
Your loves, your hates, your feelings, your country
The blackness sweeps over the whiteness of the day,
The dryness evaporates the waters of your tears.
The trees are anchored in the earth,
Away from the phantoms of your smiles;
But open, unprotected from your machines
Which tear the flesh from the bones of the earth,
Which break the skeletons asunder
Into fragmented fossil bones.
On the outskirts of your greedy cities,
Along the dust of your throbbing highways,
On the edges of your secret desires for destruction,
We live unsafe lives in your violence
Born from a latent hatred for our very skin
Covering the gentleness existing on the outskirts of your aggression.

Encapsulated

I

Once we wanted bread, you gave us indigestible stone;
Once we wanted bread, collected by our own hands:
Our paradise was in our being,
Our being was our paradise.

II

We were shameless,
They came and gave us shame;
We were innocent,
They came and gave us guilt.

III

Once our brains were fluid with thoughts;
Once our brains moved with the world;
Once our minds were unbounded as the land,
The sky was our resting place,
Our minds the sky of our brains.
Now we are marked by roads
Leading to towns of congealed thought;
Now our brains are laid out neatly;
Now our thoughts cannot wander;
But must keep to the highways which lead
To the imposed capital cities of their states of mind;
Even the skyways of our going lead straight on
Surveyed by the unswerving thoughts of their aeroplanes.

IV

Where are the roads we must follow?
Here they are, laid straight out,
Tarred and cemented, sticky with distant goals.
Where are those goals we must reach?
Here they are, thickly bound in this book.
Where are our souls which we must lead?
Here, in this church, strong-walled as a prison cell.

Reincarnation

Phoenix scars ashes of your drunkenness,
Blind hand-shakes terror of old birthing the new,
Dark skins glisten sleek with the ancient newly founded heroes,
Fast furious crackerjacks flaring us into the skies of the lawcourts
As we dream dreams of a long ago cricket team off to foreign shores,
Cold and dismal, bereft of gum trees and denuded of the oak.
Treading these ways, mates, treading these ways while splattering
Our sadness on women seeking in our lives something to add to a meaning.
Mates, our hands and feet lash out at our lack of fullness,
Our fists make deeper gaps as our moment's enemies go down –
To rise in the complete lack of a glowing victory of completion,
Even though we clothe our emptiness in quality suits and ties;
Even though our eyes reach the sun in our highest leap,
Which misses the golden moon shining with the old lost to the new.

The Death of a Poet

Robert Walker murdered at Freeo, 28 August 1984

Jungle bloomed into desert,
Wilting, deserted when Mr Walker came to the city,
Handcuffed to the cause of justice,
Shackled to the cause of injustice.
Mr Walker was given a new home in a new jungle,
Sandstone blocks turned lush with concrete vegetation,
Watered with the blood of sudden flashes of rebellion.

The story is glanced over in New Guinea and Tanzania,
Read in the skull cave, bat cave and even the lairs of the super rich,
But never do they see Mr Walker as a black man, the native,
The pygmy, clad in a grass skirt ugh ughing the trees,
Imagine my surprise when I met him in his concrete cave,
Facing out towards the sea howling a freedom gone astray,
Then I found Mr Walker beneath the mask of his father's choosing,
To be a blackman through and far beneath the flesh.

Mr Walker beneath his mask was young and black,
Frightened of all the phantoms they had made,
Made to scream his screams as they pulled him down,
His head thudding from landing stair to landing stair;
His mask shattering from landing stair to landing stair.
They dragged him down, unmasked the hero in a rage,
Finding his bare black face wishing for their death,
Finding his bare black face twisted in a white terror-stricken.

Now the ghost he walks, and talks;
Now the ghost he walks, and stalks,
Those stony corridors staggering with masked attempts,
And his screams choke off from his smashed skull,
As he seeks to rip those masks away from pain.
Mr Walker when they battered him dead,
Fled from the phantoms of his terrors,
Terrors that remained as real as the masks unreal;
Terrors that remained as real as his broken skull,
As his shattered face and smothered justice cries.

I've Met Them All

I've met them all, green and black and white.
The greeny said that he had come from earth
And had overshot the stars,
But the metho had turned his body bad,
He struck a match and went out as a fire.

The black one was a woman urgent with loves and hates,
She cried over the sins of all humankind,
Sang a female song in keeping with these times,
Then tried to convert me to a faith red with menstrual blood.

The white bloke knew every answer,
To every question I never asked,
I winked at him and grinned a drunken grin,
And said I was off to see a childhood friend.

I've met them all, green and black and white,
And all of them talked and none of them thought,
That I had the answer I never sought
In sitting and waiting as the billy boiled,
Watching the flames flickering with a thousand forms
Of soft life whispering in the scrub around,
As my mate passed the smoke over to me.

Peaches and Cream

You like peaches and cream,
And white bodies made urgent
With a flare of injustice;
You talk of oppression and hate,
And are often written up in newspapers,
While those who know you
Talk of your liking of Bundy-and-Coke,
And porno movies made
For the touches of peaches and cream gone commercial.

You hide parts of your life in superior flats,
Then wander proud into a black hotel
As if you owned the place, maybe you do,
But you stutter in your words,
And the drover's hat sits askew on your head.

You talked and talked like a white fellow,
Till the gins grew tired,
And said you raved out of your head.
Then you swore retirement,
And how it hurt, no unity
In your fight for us fought on
Till your health suffered
In too many Bundies-and-Coke,
And peaches and cream,
Which you ate with little compassion.

Last night I saw you on the telly,
Projecting Jesus and his message,
Perhaps one day I'll understand,
Though many didn't and called you hypocrite;
But they didn't know
That even Christian peaches and cream
May be sweet with a taste of injustice,
And try to sweeten it more with you.

Dreaming

Bodies entwine to make the place holy,
Ready for the ascent of the spirit.
All life is sacred, a decision to come forth.
Ovum and sperm uniting into being is a myth,
A false decision to keep or destroy material.
Nurture and let the essence swell,
Shapeless at first, soft and needing,
Green with all the wonder of increase,
Wrapt in an ageless past pressing into the present,
Entering into bodies making sacred the moment,
And allowing the spirit to take up residence
And give great presence to the future.

When I Think Of You

When I think of you,
Skin as dark as heaven,
Containing the light
I emit.

When I think of you,
Radiance absorbing my sight,
Darkness absorbing my mind,
I begin to see how things are.

Sun pours down on us;
Sun pours down on us,
Dazzled by its darkness,
What need for night.

When I think of you,
Heat drives out chilly
Thoughts of cold distant lands:
Thank Wandjina for the sun;
Thank Wandjina for warming rain;
Thank Wandjina for his hollow eyes,
Sheltering us while living and dying,
And dead.

Cat Love

Cat loving me,
I thinking it does,
Maybe?
Rubbing its body
Against parts of me,
Forcing itself into my mind.
Thinking it loves,
Why else this fuss,
I'd feed it anyway.
Have I a loving cat,
Black and freedom-loving?
Touch it – often claws;
Touch it – often purrs:
This is the only love
I have to know,
Claws and all,
A soft body in my lap.

Suntan Cream

White women on TV,
Dark men in massage parlours,
Brown as a sunny day woman,
She possessed my mind –
To leave it for cream flowing
Over pinkish bodies baking to a brown.
Star-shining eyes, better-thing soul,
Not an application of suntan cream
Over white bodies vacant of her brown.
My body was never white,
Yellow in winter, brown in summer,
What colour beneath the camouflage?
Remembering you in the seasons,
Remembering you in the feeling of the seasons,
Drifting me from yellow to brown and back again;
Remembering you reaching for tinsel stars,
Marking out the ground on which I trod.

Lost in the Lucky Country

Lost in the lucky country,
Make it from one place to the next;
Welfare's money welcome,
Though I can kill a kangaroo,
Make the flesh real tasty,
Cook the tail as stew,
Wonder why the cars don't stop,
When I walk on down the road?
Life's not worth a cent, mate,
Though in my time I've made a bob or two,
As unskilled labour,
Now they're after something else,
And all I am is handy with my hands.

I find my clean jeans at the Salvos,
They throw in a shirt or two,
And my socks don't stink,
And my boots have soles,
To move me from this place to the next,
With an accent gone awry,
So that I talk like some kind of wog,
Once someone even called me 'Yank!'
And I told him quick-smart –
We own the country now
So don't get uppity,
Or we'll bring you to your knees
And make you all Abos in a new state called free.

I Like Me City Tracks

I like me city tracks, can follow 'em in me sleep,
Get on a bus at the corner, go on until the end,
Don't need a car to get me where I want to be.
Another track, another corner, another place to go,
Get on a tram,
Destination plain to see, it's writ on the front,
Don't need a car to where I'm goin' to,
Got me a tram, bus or a train.
Don't need the wide open spaces,
Don't need a land that's scared,
Don't need a thousand dollars and too much more,
To move where I want to move where I'm goin' to be:
If you want a place where the poor can live,
Maybe the city's a better bet than home sweet home.

Don't Live in the Sand

Me mum used to tell me a 'ell of a time ago:
Don't live in the sand!
So wot 'appens,
The town cop puts in an appearance,
Tells me mum, ''E 'as to go
To that city squattin' in the sand.'
Me mum she cried, as if they'd understand:
''E can't live in that sand.'
It was no use, they put me on a train,
And sure enough, the tracks they led,
Led to that city in the sand.
There, they made me study the bible,
Said it was for me own good,
Make a Christian out of an 'eathen and all that.
I read that book, an' guess wot I find,
All writ out for kid's eyes to see and ponder:
If you want to settle, don't do it in the sand.
So naturally, seein' that me mum and God thought the same,
I took their advice and ran from the sand.
Years went by on solid ground
An' memory forgot those words of mum and God,
An' where do you think I find meself,
But livin' on the sand.
It drags me feet, an' I tracks it into the 'ouse,
An' me wife, bless her 'eart, she complains:
'Why did you bring me to the sand?'
It fills me mind as I try for a song,
It clogs me fingers when I reach for a chord:
You may find pride in bein' a sandgroper,
But as for me, I 'ates livin' in the sand.

They Have the Words,
We Have the Actions

They write books about everything these days,
Make it a course, study it in the inhumanversity.
Saw me favourite movie on telly the other day,
Go On Make My Day, I like it a lot,
Clint Eastwood is grouse, sometimes I feel a bit like him;
But wait, you don't like a thing till you've read about it in a book,
Without even a picture to relieve the squinty-eyed small print.
I listen to me favourite group, Forget The Name,
Their beat gets me and the words they follow along,
I even can play their tunes on me old guitar –
But wait, I don't know a blessed thing,
Got to read all about them in a book,
Without even the music, I missed a minor chord there.
Take a walk down Hay Street, they add Mall now,
And naturally, it's all set out in a book
With even diagrams on how to walk,
And other things, you can't guess 'em,
Well, cutting short a story, I find me a nice little lady,
Takes 'er back to the place I call me 'ome,
But you'll wait a long time to find out what 'appened:
She told me she had to read about it in a book.

Fuck it, what am I going to do with this day?
Woke up shitty in the later afternoon in no sort of mood.
Guess I'll write a poem,
Hey, wait on, they're out there,
Great big pens, all with a university degree.
Well, out to the pub for a tinny or few,
Drink them down and light up a smoke,
Lie around – nothing on the telly.
Guess it is time for a poem.
Maybe I'll write about a tree,
How it pushes out of the ground
Trying just to touch the sky,
Maybe I won't, trees have voices
And they talk to me –
Tell about how they suck the earth
And make it grow into branches and leaves
Moving gently in a courtship,
Bringing sky to ground
In a sweet magic glowing
Which causes a gentle sweetness
Way below where we can't see,
A spell of sweetness in oneness,
Making the God on high
Yearn for a lost love,
His earth mother turning into a tree.

Man or Woman

Man or woman, what did you give me?
A naked blade at midnight,
The lack of a choice to cut my own throat.
Man or woman, what did you give me?
Not even a pistol to fire the bullet
Into my defenceless brain.
Man or woman, what did you give me?
Not even flowers to perfume,
To douse the animal smell of my body.
What did you give me?
A paddock without grass,
No hands to feel my ribs,
No earth to feed my hopes.
Man or woman, what did you give me?
A soft mind to feel the pain
Of my slaughter, of my end.
What did you give me, but the dart
Of the tranquilliser gun –
Angel dust intoxicates, makes you mad
In a frenzy of panic.
Man or woman, what did you give me?
Barren skies over a barren plain.
When I too am gone, will you miss me,
In your polluted domes of plastic?

Someone Should Shoot Me

Someone should shoot me –
Watching the world flow,
Cutting down the trees,
Culling all the animals;
Someone should shoot me,
Crying over a tree,
Weeping when they kill, not me,
But my kangaroos, my buffaloes,
My donkeys and my fetishes –
All destroying the economy.

Someone should kill me,
Make me a victim to your
Painful sufferings inflicted
On my half blinded eyes;
Painful in your multiple destructions
Of brothers and sisters
In different skins and called animals.
A kangaroo hops, staggers, dies
Painfully
In your economic world,
From which we are excluded,
Though, never asking to join,
We are going, going,
Soon we shall not be found,
Except in the pages of your books,
Hymning a past age of our destruction.

Poem

When we see what we believe in;
When we see what we think;
When we see what we feel,
Then the promised land shall be ours,
Then the promised land shall be ours.

I came with a smirk, a terror mask,
Fashioned from the things I had seen,
Corpses and subjects of pain
Congealed in 'Been there, done that,'
Then I met you with a smile, 'Been there, done that,'
While beriding the earth as an endurance test:
'Been there, done that,' or –
Something somehow escapes my grasp
In these words of rhythm flowing along:
'Been there, done that!'

I hated the clown
With his cliché smile and his cliché heart,
Clichéd being in The Show Must Go On,
And then I met you and the clown
Became the clichéd real of an aching heart
Beneath the clichéd antics stirring to please;
Been there, done that: the fate of a clown;
Been there, done that: the fate of a clown.

Poem Two

They shall hate me at the waterfall;
They shall crucify me on the hill;
They shall mock me with a crown of thorns;
They shall fake my passion in their play.

They shall take my body, turn it into bread;
They shall take my blood, say that it is wine;
They shall take my heart, enthrone it;
They shall plaster it with gore;
They shall take all that I stood for,
Throw it on the floor.

They shall take my words and honour them;
They shall take my words to testify;
They shall love me in the morning,
Regret me by the afternoon.

They shall take my bones, display them;
They shall sell them at the pool,
Where I raised Lazarus, exchanging life for death.

Where I raised Lazarus, exchanging life for death;
Where I raised Lazarus, exchanging life for death;
Where they crucify me, exchanging death for life;
Where they crucify me, exchanging death for life.

Me Daddy

Me daddy was a righteous man,
That is what me mummy told me,
Tried to build up a farm,
Tried to sell his crop –
And they said:
Hey Jacky, hey Jacky,
What you trying to do,
The silo is full and yet you
Cart your grain down here.
Hey Jacky, hey Jacky,
Sell us your wheat,
We'll give you sugar and tea,
Instead of whiteman's coin,
Which you can't count.
Hey Jacky, hey Jacky,
Give us your grain,
And when you fail,
We'll understand,
And know you can't comprehend,
That money is the boss,
In the land we took from you.

Lines Written on the First Death Anniversary of Robert Marley, 11 May 1982

He died a year ago,
They always have new and secret weapons,
Our nightmares only add to their dreams,
Created from anger at our civilisation.
We formed this earth and tended it,
All they saw was a land to tame or destroy,
We made it holy, holy for their sacrilege.
You may believe something in your savage minds,
But what does God believe for you belittling a girl gone wrong?
What did you do for her before her body erupted
Into the sore, you term life?
She wanted to be cured, she wanted love,
You made her some sort of cause,
Fighting it over on government floors
She never trod except for the family court.
You had the power, she had the sore,
Your ugliness caused the earth to bleed and abort:
You killed a noble life threatening you.
Jesus is something you sing about in suits and ties,
While burning heathens who taught compassionate love.
I know your history, reading it from the records of my cells,
While remembering that fifteen-year-old girl,
Whom you saw less than dirt until she became your cause,
And you found joy in feeling the scabs of your own sores.
You teach us that Jesus means the end of wars,
Then forget us in our scores,
Just souls for your endless sacrifice.
Marx might have taught something more,
Though it caused too many bloody wars;
But still they crucify our world,
And use us as soldiers to commit their crimes.
Today, we remember Marley, who wanted something more,
Set to music, love to shout and sing about,
Stirring it up in the faces of a bored elite.
We mightn't have doctors and lawyers,
We have singers with a song,
Men and women with justice as a guide,
And a flag, not the red, white and blue.

Did Wandjina mark out this land,
Did he, did they – tell me this?
Did Wandjina mark out this land,
Did he, did they tell us to live entire,
Did he, did they? – Yes, he did!
Well, what is this Christian god,
Teaching us to rape the earth,
Separate ourselves and rape the earth,
Lose our manhood as we rip our mother,
Did Wandjina mark out his land,
Did they, what is this domination then,
This conquering, this power, this individuality?
Didn't Wandjina mark out this earth –
Who changed it, who changed it?
What is this Christian god,
What is this domination of puny humans?
When they die to whom do they return;
When they die how shall they face
Wandjina who marked out this land,
Didn't he, didn't they? – he did!

Glossary

ALLP – Australian Labor and Liberal Party.

Angel Dust – Animal tranquilliser.

Ashoka (Asoka) – Historical and mythical emperor of India, archetype of the righteous ruler (cakravartin).

Babylon – The Western World.

Bakhura – A flesh-eating demon.

Balayang – Aboriginal mythical ancestor of the Bat totem.

Boong – Contemptuous term for Aborigine.

Boro ground – a circular ceremonial ground.

Bunjil – Aboriginal mythical ancestor of the Eaglehawk totem, south-eastern Australia.

Bunurong – Koori tribe of south-eastern Australia.

Capital Hill – Site of the new Parliament house in Canberra. The site was occupied for a short time by Aboriginal youth in 1980.

CPC – Communist Party of China.

Deogam – Poet of the Ho people of India.

Devi – Literally goddess, honorific in Bengal for unmarried woman.

Dreaming – Aboriginal spiritual experience of wholeness and connection.

Folsom – United States penitentiary.

Gin – Derogatory term for Aboriginal woman.

GMA – General Motors America.

GMH – General Motors Holden, Australian subsidiary of GMA.

Goomee – Alcoholic, drinker of methylated spirits.

Govinda – Another name of the Indian diety, Krishna.

Gubba – White person.

Gunyah – An Aboriginal house.

Harijan – 'Children of God', title given by Mahatma Gandhi to the Untouchables of India, now seen as derogatory by them.

Ho – Tribal people of India.

Jacky – Once equivalent to a Quisling, now often extended in a joking fashion to all Aboriginal men. Female equivalent, Mary.

Kali (Kalima) – Black mother goddess of India.

Koori – Aboriginal person of south-eastern Australia.

Krishna – Black god of India.

Kurdaitcha (Kurdaitja) Man – Clever man, magician, Aboriginal intellectual.

Kwinkan – Spirit beings, Cape York, Queensland.

Lakh – 100 000 (rupees).

Mahatmaji – Honorific, Great Soul, in reference to M. K. Gandhi.

Marley, Robert (Bob) – Jamaican committed singer and musician advocating equal rights and justice for all.

Mimi – Thin, sticklike, spirit beings.

Minjerribah – Stradbroke Island, Queensland.

NAC – National Aboriginal Congress now abolished.

NADOC Day – National Aboriginal Day of Celebration.

Nembaluk – Aboriginal fighter of the Northern Territory.

Nunkanbah – Aboriginal settlement in Western Australia where the people stood and fought against mining on their land.

Purnima – Indian female name.

Raga – Indian musical composition.

Rani – Indian female name (Queen).

Rastaman – Member of Jamaican religious sect who believe that the last Emperor of Ethiopia was a 'Living God'. Bob Marley was an adherent of this sect.

Salvo – Salvation Army.

San Quentin – United States penitentiary.

Sanyasi – One who has renounced the world.

Sitar – Indian plucked string instrument similar to guitar.

Tamboura – Indian plucked string instrument used as a drone.

Trugernanna/Trugernanni – Famous Tasmanian Aboriginal woman who witnessed the decimation of her people at the hands of the European invaders of her island.

Unguru – Creative serpent, often called the Rainbow snake.

Walker, Robert – Aboriginal poet. His first collection *Up Not Down Mate*, was well received by the Aboriginal community. He was beaten to death by prison officers in Fremantle Prison. They were subsequently exonerated.

Wandjina – Ancestral creative beings in North-western Australia.

Worru – Dying old man in Jack Davis's drama, *The Dreamers*.

Wurley – A temporary shelter.

Yama – The Hindu God of Death.

Index of First Lines